Every Day with Jesus

NOV/DEC 2018

Strong at the Broken Places

'My grace is sufficient for you, for my power is made perfect in weakness.' 2 Corinthians 12:9

Selwyn Hughes
Revised and updated by Mick Brooks

© CWR 2018. Dated text previously published as *Every Day with Jesus: Strong at the Broken Places* (November/December 2005) by CWR. This edition revised and updated for 2018 by Mick Brooks.

CWR, Waverley Abbey House, Waverley Lane, Farnham, Surrey GU9 8EP, UK **Tel: 01252 784700**
Email: mail@cwr.org.uk Registered Charity No. 294387. Registered Limited Company No. 1990308.

Cover image: Adobestock.com
Quiet Time image: Adobestock.com
Printed in England by Linney

MIX
Paper from
responsible sources
FSC® C015900

CWR

Every Day with Jesus is available in large print from CWR. It is also available on **audio and DAISY** in the UK and Eire for the sole use of those with a visual impairment worse than N12, or who are registered blind. For details please contact **Torch Trust for the Blind**, Tel: 01858 438260. Torch House, Torch Way, Northampton Road, Market Harborough LE16 9HL.

A word of introduction...

I remember it clearly: it was 2006 when I was diagnosed with prostate cancer, and the news propelled me into one of those 'I didn't see that coming' moments, which can sneak up and take us by surprise. Perhaps that's been your experience recently? As 2018 draws to a close, we explore together how, with God's help, we can find strength even at the lowest and most broken points of our lives.

The theme of this issue reminds me of the ancient Japanese art of kintsugi – which translates as 'golden repair' – where broken pottery is fixed with a special lacquer dusted with powdered gold, silver, or platinum. Beautiful seams of gold glint in the cracks of ceramic ware, giving a unique appearance to the piece. This repair technique celebrates each artefact's unique history by emphasising its fractures and breaks instead of hiding or disguising them. Kintsugi often makes the repaired piece even more beautiful than the original, revitalising it with new life. It seems such an appropriate metaphor for the transforming hope of our God, who can take what was meant for harm and use it to turn our broken places into a source of strength.

As human beings we are mostly self-sufficient and self-reliant, meaning that it often takes the occurrence of something beyond our ability to control or handle, before we turn to God for His help, guidance and comfort. But when we are weak, we know His strength. He takes our brokenness and makes it into something beautiful. I pray you will know that truth this issue.

Mick Brooks, Consulting Editor

Free small group resource to accompany this issue can be found at **www.cwr.org.uk/extra**

The *EDWJ* Facebook community is growing!
To join the conversation visit **www.facebook.com/edwjpage**

Turning weakness to strength

FOR READING & MEDITATION – HEBREWS 11:30–40

'whose weakness was turned to strength; and who became powerful in battle' (v34)

The theme now about to engage our attention is the way in which God is able to take the struggles of His people and turn them into strengths. What an exciting and liberating truth! The writer to the Hebrews, in today's reading, gives us a long list of people whose negative experiences God turned into positives. So our subject matter has a good biblical foundation.

In *A Farewell to Arms*, Ernest Hemingway wrote that although the world breaks everyone, 'many are strong at the broken places'. Hemingway was drawing attention to the fact that some people are able to recover from the experience of feeling broken and go on to be stronger than they were before. The human spirit can rise to great heights when faced with trauma and trouble, and there are multitudes of people who, though not committed Christians, draw on their inner strength to survive and recover from the most devastating experiences. The exciting thing about the Christian life, however, is that whether or not we are temperamentally gifted with a strong fighting spirit, we are able to draw on the redemptive gift of grace from God and every weakness can be turned into strength. There is nothing that happens to us which cannot be transformed by God into good. This is what happens as we place ourselves into God's hands.

FURTHER STUDY

Gen. 45:1–8; Psa. 62:1–4, 11–12

1. How did God transform Joseph's experience?

2. On what two truths does the psalmist rely?

Has something happened recently in your life to bring you to a place of spiritual or psychological struggle? Has it left you feeling woefully weak and inadequate? Then take heart – God specialises in matching His ability to your disability. By His transforming grace, your frustration can become fruitful. You can be strong at the broken places.

Father, this sounds wonderful in theory, but can it be true in fact? Your Word says it can. What You have done for others You can do also for me. I am eager to experience it. Grant that it may be so. In Jesus' name. Amen.

Toughening under adversity

FOR READING & MEDITATION – PSALM 28:1–9

'The LORD is the strength of his people, a fortress of salvation for his anointed one.' (v8)

Often in life something happens that causes us to almost break apart, but at the same time strengthens us so that we are better prepared to face a similar situation in the future. A visitor to the Netherlands tells how his guide pointed out a historic site. 'This is where once the sea broke through,' the guide said, 'and caused untold damage, also bringing about the deaths of hundreds of people. But see – now the breach has been dealt with in such an effective way that one doubts whether it could happen again.' Some Christians, however, when broken by difficult or traumatic circumstances, never seem to recover, and remain in a constant state of struggle rather than strength. Why? I think the following illustration might help provide part of the answer.

FURTHER STUDY

Matt. 14:25–32;
John 15:1–8

1. What did Peter need to hold on to?

2. What does Jesus promise if we remain in Him?

A writer who lived in India describes how he sat on his veranda one day and noticed a vine that had reached its delicate tendrils up and across a void until it had grasped the branch of a pine tree. That night there was a fierce storm. The following morning, the vine had become a poor drooping thing, with its stems hanging downwards because the branch to which it had been clinging had broken in the storm. The vine had fastened upon a rotting branch instead of the strong, healthy trunk.

There are some Christians who fasten themselves upon something other than Jesus – a denomination, a religious rite, a custom, or even a person. A storm comes and down they go, because they fastened on to the culture surrounding Jesus rather than Jesus Himself. When men and women hold on to the central reality – Jesus – they strengthen, rather than sag, under adversity.

Lord Jesus, how I long for You to become my one steady place in a world full of flux and change. Help me to fasten on to You and not on to the things that are connected with You. For Your own dear name's sake. Amen.

'Cosmic optimism'

FOR READING & MEDITATION – ACTS 13:13–25

'God... made the people prosper during their stay in Egypt' (v17)

Yesterday we were saying that one of the reasons why some Christians are not made strong at the broken places is because they latch on to something connected to Jesus, rather than on to Jesus Himself. Certain Christians hold more tightly to a particular doctrine than they do to Christ. Then, when a storm comes, they go down with it because they are not fastened to the central trunk.

The Revised Standard Version translates today's text like this: 'God... made the people great during their stay in the land of Egypt.' When we look at the history of the children of Israel in Egypt, we might wonder how they were made 'great', but that is what the Scripture says. We can speculate on the various ways in which 'greatness' was achieved, but one thing is clear: the adversity they went through toughened them and prepared them for their deliverance.

FURTHER STUDY

Exod. 3:11–15;
Jer. 29:4–7;
Rom. 8:31–37

1. On what could Moses rely?

2. What 'cosmic optimism' does Paul display?

The truth I want us to grasp in this issue is that although we accept that sometimes life threatens to break us, we also accept that we can become strong at the broken places. Everything can be redeemed. Christianity has been described by some as 'cosmic optimism'. There is redemptive vitality available to change the course of our lives that provides direction and choice. It is true that there are limitations under the present conditions in this world, for there are other wills that attempt to thwart us as well as our recalcitrant human nature. But ultimately we are not limited by those limitations. With God they can be turned into contributions. Be assured of this: nothing can work successfully against us in the long term when we have God on our side. Nothing.

Father, how can we sufficiently thank You for the hope that You put within us when we are linked with You and the other members of the Trinity? Your dependability makes life worth living. Amen.

The scars on optimism

FOR READING & MEDITATION – LUKE 14:15–24

'Then the master told his servant, "Go out to the roads and country lanes and make them come in"' (v23)

We mentioned yesterday that Christianity has been described by some as 'cosmic optimism'. However, one writer goes on to say that 'it is an optimism with scars on it'. I believe this person has in mind the truth that, although in Christ we have the promise that He will turn all the bad things in life that come our way to good, we need to accept that there will still be some things that frustrate us.

For example, the Scriptures say that after the temptation, 'Jesus returned to Galilee in the power of the Spirit' (Luke 4:14). That gives a picture of Jesus with tremendous power to heal the sick and captivate the minds of men and women with the words He spoke. Yet at one point He had to confess that 'a prophet has no honour in his own country' (John 4:44). Imagine it – the Saviour, out of whom came supernatural power, was prevented from working in His home town because of unbelief (Matt. 13:58)!

The seed may be sound but its fruitfulness depends on the soil and other conditions. So, as we have already said, there are limitations and matters that will hinder and frustrate us in this fallen world. But the exciting thing is that with Jesus we can overcome even the things that obstruct us. With God's help, if we can't get through something, often we can get around it.

When, in the parable we have read today, the invited guests turned down their invitation to the banquet, the servant was told to go out into the streets and alleys of the town and persuade all and sundry to come in. Obstruction became the opportunity for universality. How wonderful.

FURTHER STUDY

Acts 11:19–24; 13:44–48

1. How was persecution turned to advantage for the Early Church?

2. How did Paul and Barnabas respond to abuse?

God my Father, what a joy it is to discover I have a faith that gives me a cosmic optimism, and a Saviour on whom I can depend to turn everything to good in my life. I am so deeply grateful. Amen.

CWR Ministry Events

PLEASE PRAY FOR THE TEAM

DATE	EVENT	PLACE	PRESENTER(S)
3 Nov	Insight into Perfectionism/ Shame	All Saints Church, Peckham	Patrick Regan and Heather Churchill
8 Nov	Hearing God's Voice	Waverley Abbey House	Andy Peck
12–16 Nov	Introduction to Biblical Care and Counselling	WAH	IBCC team
14 Nov	Preaching with Humour	WAH	Andy Peck
16 Nov	Healthy You, Healthy School	WAH	Derek Holbird
20 Nov	Advent Supper	WAH	Philip Greenslade
28 Nov	Every Day with God: Arranging Life around God's Purposes	WAH	Andy Peck
28 Nov	Great Chapters of the Bible	WAH	Philip Greenslade
29 Nov	Changing Your Life as God Intends	WAH	Andy Peck
5 Dec	Revolutionise Your Devotional Life	WAH	Andy Peck
6 Dec	Inspiring Women Christmas Celebration	WAH	Elizabeth Hodkinson and the Inspiring Women team

Please pray for our students and tutors on our ongoing BA Counselling programme at Waverley Abbey College (which takes place at Waverley Abbey House), as well as our Certificate in Christian Counselling and MA Counselling qualifications.

We would also appreciate prayer for our ongoing ministry in Singapore and Cambodia, as well as the many regional events that will be happening around the UK this year.

For further information and a full list of CWR's courses, seminars and events, call **(+44) 01252 784719** or visit **www.cwr.org.uk/courses**

You can also download our free Prayer Track, which includes daily prayers, from **www.cwr.org.uk/prayertrack**

'But from now on'

FOR READING & MEDITATION – LUKE 22:63–71

'But from now on, the Son of Man will be seated at the right hand of the mighty God.' (v69)

In his book *A Confession*, the writer Leo Tolstoy talks about different attitudes to life that can be found among people. Tolstoy proposes that there are those who say: (1) life is bad, so get drunk to evade and forget it; (2) life is bad, so do the logical thing – end it; (3) life is bad, but go on living, accepting life as it comes. None of these approaches have any parallels to the life God had in mind for His creation. In God we do not merely accept life as it comes, but we use the resources He gives to make life what it was originally meant it to be.

FURTHER STUDY

Acts 7:54–60;
9:1–6

1. How did Stephen experience a sense of immediacy?

2. How did Paul catch the immediacy of Christ's power?

Over the past few days we have been saying that the Christian outlook could be defined as 'cosmic optimism'. Many of you, I know, would prefer the word 'hope' as it is a more biblical word, so if the word 'optimism' bothers you then think of it as being synonymous with hope. Edward Burroughs, an American writer, says, 'Christianity combines the most absolute pessimism about man's unaided powers with an unquenchable optimism as to what in God's hands it may become.'

If there ever was a moment when Jesus could have felt pessimism, it was when He was standing before the Sanhedrin. Before the formal session, the guards had struck Him in the face, blindfolded Him, spat upon Him, and yet despite all this He stood and said, 'But from now on, the Son of Man will be seated at the right hand of the mighty God.' With both hands bound, He talks about God turning the tables. He did not say, 'It will happen one day'. Instead He said, 'But from now on'. He brought it into the here and now. We too can learn to catch the immediacy of Jesus: 'But from now on.' Bringing it into the present is the way forward.

Father, I am so grateful for this sense of immediacy. You take the broken things of life and bring them into the here and now. Hallelujah! Amen.

Afraid of sanity

FOR READING & MEDITATION – LUKE 8:26–39

'Then all the people of the region... asked Jesus to leave them, because they were overcome with fear.' (v37)

Now we turn our attention to some of the ways in which life may break us and what we can do to become 'strong at the broken places'. First let's consider the issue of shattered hopes, plans and disappointment. This is often a difficult issue to face because of the frustration we feel when the plans we have made for our life come to nothing.

Consider how Jesus responded to the rejection of His plans in the incident recorded in today's reading. After He had healed the demon-possessed man, the people who lived locally came to see what had happened. When they found the man 'sitting at Jesus' feet, dressed and in his right mind' we read, 'they were overcome with fear'. What were they afraid of – sanity? The people begged Jesus to leave the area. His presence had cost them too much. Here was a man who was prepared to sacrifice a herd of pigs in order to deliver a man possessed by demons. I wonder if their fear was due partly to the fact that they couldn't understand Jesus. We can often be afraid of something we do not understand. Were they afraid that He might do something else to upset their values?

FURTHER STUDY

Acts 16:6–10, 25–34

1. How did God change Paul's plans?

2. How did God redirect Paul's ministry?

How did Jesus respond to this rejection? He simply turned in another direction. His ministry was not so much rejected as redirected. If you read the rest of the chapter, and the one that follows, you will see that Jesus then performed some of His greatest miracles. He turned the blocking into a blessing. The frustration turned to fruitfulness. When our plans and hopes are shattered, we learn to do what Jesus did: receive the grace that constantly flows towards you from God and consider turning in another direction.

Father, whenever my plans are frustrated, help me understand that there is a purpose in what is happening. Sometimes plans upset me in order to set me up – to set me up with new and better plans. I am so grateful. Amen.

Isolation becomes revelation

FOR READING & MEDITATION – REVELATION 1:9–20

'a loud voice... said: "Write on a scroll what you see and send it to the seven churches"' (vv10–11)

Yesterday we saw that the ministry of Jesus was not deterred by opposition. Turning in another direction, He was able to work some of His greatest miracles – for example, the feeding of the five thousand. The deflection became for Him a spur. I wonder, am I talking to someone who is feeling defeated because much of what you planned has gone wrong? Whatever you are feeling right now can be turned into strength by the grace of God that is flowing towards you.

When John was banished to the island of Patmos because of his allegiance to Jesus, it must have seemed that his ministry and his plans had all been cruelly and abruptly ended. He says: 'I, John... was on... Patmos because of the word of God and the testimony of Jesus. On the Lord's Day I was in the Spirit, and I heard behind me a loud voice like a trumpet, which said: "Write... what you see..."' (Rev. 1:9–11). So, isolated from other Christians and prevented from ministering to them by word of mouth, John wrote what he saw, and as a result blessed not only the churches of his day but the whole Christian Church from that day to this!

John's isolation became a place of revelation. In a lesser way, the failure of our plans can be an opportunity for us to stop and listen to see if God is leading in a different direction. Whenever my plans were shattered I would first pray and confess any self-centredness. Then I would write out whatever I felt the Spirit was showing me. It would take a while to discern but eventually it became clear. Can I encourage you today, if your plans have gone wrong, to listen to what God is saying – and write!

FURTHER STUDY

1 Kings 19:13–18; Jer. 26:12–16

1. What plans did God reveal to Elijah in his isolation?

2. What vision was Jeremiah true to, even when threatened with death?

Gracious and loving heavenly Father, it is Your purposes I want to achieve, not my own. Whenever my own self-centred plans are crossed, help me to discover Your better plans. In Jesus' name. Amen.

Working with a wound

FOR READING & MEDITATION – MATTHEW 14:1–14

'The king was distressed, but... he ordered that her request be granted and had John beheaded in the prison.' (vv9–10)

Today we continue reflecting on the thought that when our plans are shattered, and we feel drained by life's seemingly bitter blows, through God's grace a new strength can enter our lives. We can be made strong at the broken places.

In today's passage Jesus had just heard that John the Baptist, His cousin and forerunner, had been beheaded. The account says: 'When Jesus heard what had happened, he withdrew by boat privately to a solitary place.' No doubt He wanted to be alone to deal with the hurt, disappointment and grief that the news of His cousin's death would undoubtedly have caused. But when word got out that Jesus had gone somewhere to be alone, a crowd followed Him to that solitary place. How did Jesus react to the fact that the people had impinged on His plans to be alone, and at a time of great pain? We read, 'he had compassion on them and healed their sick' (v14).

FURTHER STUDY

2 Cor. 1:3–7; 1 Pet. 2:21–25

1. In what ways is God the 'God of all comfort'?

2. How does Peter say we have been healed?

Many of you, I imagine, will respond to this by saying: 'Well, that was Jesus. We can't be expected to respond in quite the same way as the Son of God.' Frequently I have explored with counsellors in training that you will begin to realise how much like Jesus you are becoming, when you can minister to others even though your heart longs for someone to minister to you. Am I saying this is easy to do? Of course not. I have failed in this respect many times myself. But it is possible. Jesus, who wore our flesh and measured its frailty, promises to be with us always. He knows what it is to be hurt and stands at our side ready to provide us with the strength we need to minister to others, even though our own heart may be broken. He gives most when most is taken away.

Lord Jesus, You who knew what it was to be wounded, help me remember that Your wounds can heal my wounds. Grant also that my wounds might heal someone else's wounds. May my hurts be healing. Amen.

Gathering up the 'remainders'

FOR READING & MEDITATION – PHILIPPIANS 4:4–13

'I can do everything through him who gives me strength.' (v13)

At present we are saying that when our plans and hopes are shattered and our dreams in tatters, God can pour His strength into our struggling soul and reconstruct our shattered plans, making them far better than they were before.

I once came across the phrase 'getting meaning out of life's remainders'. Sometimes life leaves us with nothing but 'remainders'. But with God's help we can gather up those 'remainders' and make meaning out of them. My father used to claim: 'When it says in the book of Revelation that there was silence in heaven for the space of half an hour, it was because God was moving the scenery for the next act.' So often the silences we experience, when our hopes are shattered and our plans seem delayed or destroyed, may be God's way of preparing you for the next act. Hold steady. God never abandons His children, and He takes a Father's interest in everything we do. It's important to remember that He hurts in our hurts.

I once talked to a person who told me he had planned with his family to emigrate and start a whole new life together in a different country. When, at the last moment, their plans fell through, he thought that he would never recover from the blow. However, within three months, with God's guidance, he found himself in a new career that took him, he said, beyond his wildest dreams. 'Now,' he remarked, 'I believe that God allowed my plans to be shattered because He had bigger and better ones for me.' When you get to the end of your rope, tie a knot and hang on. Help is on the way, in the presence of Jesus Himself and backed up with the full resources of heaven.

FURTHER STUDY

Psa. 40:1–8; Rom. 8:23–27

1. What happened when the psalmist waited patiently?

2. What help can we receive as we wait patiently?

Father, I feel my heart filling up with the 'cosmic optimism' we reflected on earlier. Help me realise that I am capable of anything through Your strength and power. For Jesus' sake. Amen.

The hidden 'better'

SAT
10 NOV

FOR READING & MEDITATION – JOHN 16:5–16

'But I tell you the truth: It is for your good that I am going away.' (v7)

We saw yesterday that the silences we experience when our plans are delayed or lie shattered could be God's way of preparing us for the next act.

How it must have confused the disciples when Jesus said He was about to leave them. After three years it looked as if His ministry was making its mark. Even though there were those who hated Him, the crowds loved Him and flocked to Him wherever He went. The disciples' hearts must have sunk when He talked about going away. They had given up their jobs to travel with Him. Peter had turned from his fishing nets, Matthew from his tax collecting. I imagine the announcement that He was leaving them brought about a collapse of all their hopes and expectations. Yet though they did not realise it at the time, what they thought was the collapse of their plans was in reality the changing of the scenery for the next act. Jesus was saying in effect: 'My going is for your good. You will lose my physical presence, but the day will come when I will not just be with you but in you. You will experience greater intimacy and know me better than you can possibly imagine – much closer than I am at this moment. You will only need to search your heart to find me there.'

FURTHER STUDY

Job 42:10–17;
Acts 2:32–36;
1 Pet. 1:8–9

1. What did the disciples realise about Jesus at Pentecost?

2. How close to Jesus can we feel as believers?

Those disciples were to learn, as you and I must learn, that God never takes away the good unless He intends to replace it with the better. After Pentecost, the disciples realised that though Jesus had gone, He was closer to them than ever through the Spirit. So let this thought become a prevailing principle in your life: your shattered plans and hopes may be just the prelude to the advancement of His.

God my Father, when some earthly good is taken away and I am left feeling bereft, help me to see the hidden 'better'. Fortify my soul with this expectation, I pray. In Jesus' name. Amen.

A day at a time

FOR READING & MEDITATION – MATTHEW 6:25–34

'do not worry about tomorrow, for tomorrow will worry about itself.'
(v34)

FURTHER STUDY

John 1:16–18;
Eph. 3:14–19

1. Through whom do we receive an endless supply of grace?

2. Pray through Paul's prayer.

Now we begin to explore another issue that can break people: stress. Some years ago, it was estimated that in the UK alone there were around 8.2 million people treated for anxiety – and many reading these notes will be among those. I regularly received letters from people who said something like this: 'I feel I'm on the verge of a breakdown. No one thing seems to be responsible for it but I just can't cope. My doctor says I'm suffering from tension and stress. My blood pressure is sky high and medication seems to do little for it. Can God help me with this?' Indeed He can – there is no one better.

At one point in my life, I lived with such stress and tension that I had a physical breakdown. In fact, as a result of that period of tension, I developed an illness which almost took my life. It came about because I considered myself the 'Director of the Universe' and took on the responsibility of helping God run His world. When I resigned from that position and began to live my life by biblical principles, I found that I had a strength I never had before. If there is one thing I have learned, and been able to pass on to others, it is how to overcome tension and stress. I have been made strong at the broken places.

Today's text was the first thing God impressed upon me. As soon as I accepted that God has so arranged life that it comes to us in manageable portions – a day at a time – my whole perspective changed. When I eventually learned to live a day at a time – shutting off yesterday and not worrying about tomorrow – a new phase of my life began which, with God's help and His endless supply of grace, continued.

Father, how I need to be reminded of this – that life is designed to be lived a day at a time. Help me understand the great importance of all this. In Jesus' name. Amen.

'Life by the inch is a cinch'

FOR READING & MEDITATION – 1 PETER 5:1–11

'Cast all your anxiety on him because he cares for you.' (v7)

One of the first things we need to learn, I believe, if we are to overcome tension and stress is, as I said yesterday, that God has arranged for life to come to us in manageable portions – a day at a time. Suppose all the future were dumped into our lap in one fell swoop. We would be overwhelmed. But our wise God has decreed that life be served up in small portions, so that anyone can manage it if he or she takes it as it is given. The worries of yesterday, plus the worries piled into today, can break the stoutest spirit. But divide your worries – and you conquer them. Someone wrote this in my Bible after I had just become a Christian:

> *I have nothing to do with tomorrow,*
> *My Saviour will make that His care,*
> *Its grace and its faith I can't borrow,*
> *So why should I borrow its care?*

Dr Robert Schuller was renowned for saying, 'Life by the yard is hard; life by the inch is a cinch.' But you might be saying to yourself: 'That's all very well, but what can I do about the worries of yesterday and those of tomorrow? I'm facing some very difficult situations.' Well, God has them in His hands. He has your yesterdays and is willing to forgive any mistakes made in them – providing, of course, that you ask Him to do so. He holds your tomorrows, too, and will provide the grace and power to meet them – but only as they come. Our heavenly Father does not provide for what is not yet here. His grace is like the manna the Israelites ate in the wilderness; when kept over for the next day (except before the Sabbath), it spoiled (see Exod. 16). It had to be eaten day by day.

FURTHER STUDY

Psa. 23:1–6;
Col. 1:9–14

1. Make Psalm 23 a personal confession of faith.

2. For what should we give thanks to the Father?

Help me, heavenly Father, to cast all my anxieties about life fully on You. You are daily bearing my burden. Plant that truth deeply into my spirit, I pray. In Jesus' name. Amen.

Causes of tension

FOR READING & MEDITATION – EXODUS 33:12–23

'The LORD replied, "My Presence will go with you, and I will give you rest."' (v14)

Why do we get so caught up in tension and stress? One answer is that we are trying to live life against itself.

A certain man known to me struggled in life because the girl he wanted to marry wouldn't agree to be his wife. His tension and consequent stress became so acute he ended up in hospital. Now if he had said, 'I want to marry this woman if it is the best thing for me, but if I can't, I will use the disappointment for higher purposes,' then he would, I believe, have avoided significant distress. In counselling we might call this type of behaviour 'demandingness'. It is the desire to have our own way even though it may not be best for us.

FURTHER STUDY

Gen. 2:2–3;
Psa. 91:1–6;
Matt. 11:27–30

1. How did the psalmist find God's rest?

2. Focus on Jesus and His promise.

Many times we become tense because we get caught up in the hectic pace of life. We think we are not achieving anything unless we are doing things in a hurry. I love this prayer, which I came across in the USA:

Slow me down, Lord, I'm going too fast,
I can't see my brother when he's walking past.
I miss a lot of good things day by day,
When they come my way.
Slow me down, Lord, I'm going too fast.

The man who accomplished most on this planet of ours was never in a hurry, never ran (as far as we can tell), never 'busied' people around, and He was never fussily busy. His whole life spells 'calm'. But oh, what a hurricane lay at the heart of all He did. Although He lived on earth for only 33 years, it's important to remember it's not the years you put in that counts: it's what you put into the years that matters.

Father, slow me down if I'm going too fast. I don't want the tension of the world to drive my life. I want life to come from You. In place of my restlessness please give me Your rest. In Jesus' name. Amen.

A Strange Christmas...

It's the same story every year – the twinkling nativity scene, our favourite carols and the familiar Bible passages read out by candlelight. But there's so much more to the Christmas story than the cleaned-up version we might have become used to.

This Advent, reflect on the seemingly bizarre circumstances around Jesus' birth from a refreshing new angle. Over 31 days, Krish Kandiah shows just how strange this wonderful and world-changing story actually is. He says:

'This Advent, I want to go on that journey again with you. I want to dig out the strange circumstances that led to the birth of Jesus, and what that means for us and our messy lives. I want to question why people responded in such ways, and what that means for the way we worship God. I want to find out why God included such strange people, and make the connection with the tough challenge of a Christmas story that constantly welcomes strangers. And I want to dig deeper into why, according to God's strange wisdom, Christmas is supposed to change everything.'

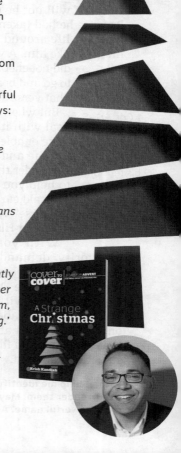

It's not too late for you to order your copy to use either on your own, or together with your small group. Order direct from **www.cwr.org.uk/shop** or by using the order form at the back of these notes. Also available in Christian bookshops.

ISBN: 978-1-78259-892-3

Surrendering your tensions

S taying with the matter of tension and stress, I heard of a preacher who eventually collapsed under the weight of pressure and tension because every time he spoke one particular verse of Scripture came before him: 'I beat my body and make it my slave so that after I have preached to others, I myself will not be disqualified for the prize' (1 Cor. 9:27). Because he had taken a verse of Scripture out of context and built his life around it, this man became so stressed that it finally broke him. A verse that always helped me is this: 'You did not choose me, but I chose you and appointed you to go and bear fruit – fruit that will last' (John 15:16). That verse sustained me more times than I can say.

FURTHER STUDY

Psa. 37:1–11;
1 Cor. 2:1–5

1. In what ways did the psalmist surrender his tensions to God?

2. 'In weakness', on what did Paul rely?

But when stress threatens to break us, how do we deal with it? Permit me to share three things that have enabled me to deal with stress and tension in my life and turn a weakness into a strength. First, surrender the point of tension to God and invite Him to help you to handle it. My great point of tension, as I said earlier, was trying to be the 'Director of the Universe'. When I surrendered that role and let God look after His own world, I was tremendously relieved.

With you the problem might be different: inferiority, demandingness, fear of what might happen, perfectionism. Please remember, you can't change what you don't acknowledge. Are you trying too hard to meet people's expectations? It will cause you endless stress. Ask yourself now: what thing above all others makes me anxious? It is only when you set about identifying the cause of your stress that you can build faith in God and ask for His help in doing something about it.

Father, help me identify the tension points in my life and be willing to surrender them. May I let go of them all. This I ask in Jesus' most powerful name. Amen.

Don't push the river

FOR READING & MEDITATION – JOHN 10:1–10

'I have come that they may have life, and have it to the full.' (v10)

The second thing I suggest we need to do to avoid being broken by life's tensions is to learn to live by relaxed receptivity. Jesus once said, 'Consider the lilies how they grow' (Luke 12:27, KJV). How does a plant grow? By getting tense and anxious? No, it grows by receptivity to earth and air and sun.

Christians who don't spend time sitting quietly in the presence of God, drawing from Him the resources that only He can provide – grace and peace – may find themselves rapidly approaching burnout. Learning to keep our channels open in order to receive is one of the most important lessons in life. J.B. Phillips translates Hebrews 13:9 in this way: 'Spiritual stability depends on the grace of God, and not on rules of diet.' It depends on what God does for us and not on what we do for Him.

The third thing we can do to overcome tension and stress is to stop being individuals who are being driven, and to get back into the driving seat ourselves. Many who suffer tension and stress are people who are being driven – driven by the expectations of others or by their own expectations. So ask yourself these questions right now: am I being driven or am I in the driving seat? Am I in control of my personality or is it in control of me? Perhaps you need to sit down and, in an attitude of prayer, begin to consider rearranging some of your priorities. From time to time it is helpful to ask these questions, because things can creep in that appear important but when looked at more critically may be less so. How much better would it be if we could ride the wave of God's blessing rather than continually untangling and relearning the consequences of living a self-dependent and not a God-dependent life.

FURTHER STUDY

Psa. 1:1–6;
Luke 10:38–42

1. What were the psalmist's priorities?

2. What was Mary's priority?

God, help me come to grips with the raw material of living so that out of it comes the person You long for me to be. Help me not to try to push the river of life – but to ride the wave. In Jesus' name. Amen.

When riches take wings

FOR READING & MEDITATION – PROVERBS 23:1–8

'Cast but a glance at riches, and they are gone, for they will surely sprout wings and fly off' (v5)

Now we move on to consider yet another way in which life can break us: through financial disaster or material loss. Some Christians speak disparagingly about money. I have heard them misquote Scripture by saying, 'Money is the root of all evil.' They forget that the text actually reads: 'The love of money is the root of all evil' (1 Tim. 6:10, KJV). Money in itself is not evil. It lends itself to a thousand philanthropies – it feeds the hungry and clothes the naked.

Some years ago, the Recorder at the Old Bailey (the Central Criminal Court in London) made a statement that was taken up by the national press and reported in almost every newspaper. He said: 'A couple of pounds very often saves a life – and sometimes a soul.' It may be true that money cannot bring happiness but, as somebody has remarked, 'it can certainly put our creditors in a better frame of mind!'

FURTHER STUDY

Jer. 9:23–24;
Luke 8:11–15

1. In what should we boast?

2. What can get in the way of seed producing a crop?

For some people there is nothing more painful than a serious financial reverse, when they experience what the writer of Proverbs describes as 'riches taking wings'. Can we be made strong at the broken place of financial failure? It is my belief that we can. I knew a man who lost all his financial assets. Such was the reverse he experienced that he lost everything – literally everything. Life broke him. However, he emerged from the experience with a new philosophy that altered his whole attitude to money. He became a competent businessman with enormous financial resources and gave liberally to Christian causes. I was sure of this: that never again would life break this man at that point. He was made strong at the broken place. And so, my friend, can you.

Father, help me over the coming days to settle once and for all my attitude towards this complex problem of money. If it is a weakness, then help me make it a strength. For Jesus' sake. Amen.

A test of discipleship

FOR READING & MEDITATION – GENESIS 22:1–19

'because you have... not withheld your son, your only son, I will surely bless you' (vv16–17)

Yesterday we mentioned a man who emerged from a financial loss with a philosophy that enabled him to say, 'Never again will I be broken by material loss.' And why? Because he developed a biblical perspective which helped him to see the whole issue of finances from God's point of view. People have frequently said to me, 'You often talk about money in *Every Day with Jesus*.' My response: 'So did Jesus.' The way we perceive money is sometimes a good measure of our dependency on God.

Here are the steps my friend took to move from money being his master to it being his servant, and to financial freedom. First, in a definite act of commitment, transfer the ownership of all your possessions to God. Whether we acknowledge it or not, we do not really own our possessions. We are stewards, not proprietors, of the assets God puts into our hands. My friend told me that after reading the story of Abraham and his willingness to sacrifice his son, he pictured himself kneeling before God's altar and offered all his possessions to the Lord. He said: 'I continued in prayer until every item I had was laid on God's altar, and when it was over, I was a changed man. That act of dedication became the transformation point as regards my finances.'

FURTHER STUDY

1 Chron. 29:10–17; Psa. 50:7–15

1. What was David's attitude to wealth and possessions?

2. What is God's attitude to sacrifices?

When we realise that we are just the stewards of our possessions, the sensible thing is to say to God: 'Lord, I'm not the owner but the ower.' When we begin to handle our possessions as belonging to God, then life becomes more meaningful. Money is no longer your master; it becomes, instead, a means of ministering.

Father, once again I ask that You help me to take a long, honest look at where I place my dependency – money or You. Grant that I might see myself as a steward and not a proprietor. Help me understand this. In Jesus' name. Amen.

'I will take its yoke'

FOR READING & MEDITATION – COLOSSIANS 3:1–17

'Set your minds on things above, not on earthly things.' (v2)

We continue looking at the steps we can take to overcome financial disaster and so become strong at this place of weakness. The second step is to position your life for the purposes of God's kingdom. Explorer and missionary David Livingstone once said: 'I will place no value on anything that I have or possess, except in relation to the kingdom of Christ. If anything I have will advance that kingdom it shall be given or kept, whichever will best promote the glory of Him to whom I owe all my hopes, both for time and eternity.' In response, another missionary said: 'That first sentence of Livingstone's should become the life motto of every Christian. Each Christian should repeat this slowly to himself every day: I will place no value on anything I have or possess, except in relation to the kingdom of Christ.' If it advances the kingdom, it has value – it can stay. We either make it useful or leave it behind.

FURTHER STUDY

Mark 10:17–23;
Acts 2:42–47

1. Why was the rich young man unwilling to streamline his life?

2. How did the Early Church advance the kingdom?

Although I've told the following story before, it bears repeating. It concerns John Wanamaker, a Christian businessman, who many years ago visited China to see if the donations he had made to missionary work were being used to their best advantage. He came to a village where there was a beautiful church, and in a nearby field he caught sight of a young man yoked together with an ox, ploughing a field. He went over and asked why there was this strange yoking. An elderly man who was driving the plough said: 'When we were trying to build the church, my son and I had no money to give, so my son said, "Let us sell one of our two oxen and I will take its yoke." We did and gave the money to the chapel.' Wanamaker wept!

Father, help me come to terms with my relationship with 'things' so that my life is much more streamlined for kingdom purposes. May I be willing to be hitched to a plough and know the joy of sacrifice. For Jesus' sake. Amen.

Lifted above all distinctions

MON
19 NOV

FOR READING & MEDITATION – PHILIPPIANS 4:10–20

*'I have learned the secret of being content in any and every situation...
whether living in plenty or in want.' (v12)*

Today we think about the third step my friend took to rebuild his life following a financial collapse: recognise that you are truly free only when you are free to use either poverty or plenty.

There are two ways in which people try to defend themselves against financial disaster. One is by saving as much as possible in an attempt to avert it. The other is by renouncing money and material things entirely in order to be free from its control. Both approaches have pitfalls. The first, because it can cause tightfistedness and anxiety, and tends to make a person as metallic as the coins they seek to amass. The second, because it seeks to get rid of the difficulty by shunning it completely. In each case there is a captivity: one is a captivity to material things; the other a captivity to poverty. Those who are free to use plenty only are bound by that, while those who are free to use poverty only are also bound. While the world is continually, through advertising, telling us, 'You'll never have enough and you'll never be satisfied,' the person who, like Paul, has 'learned the secret of being content... whether living in plenty or in want' is free – really free.

A missionary who was once waiting for a train in India, engaged a high-caste Indian in conversation. 'Are you travelling on the next train?' the missionary asked. 'No,' he replied, 'that train has only third class carriages. It's all right for you because you are a Christian. Third class doesn't degrade you and first class doesn't exalt you. You are above these distinctions, but I have to observe them.' Lifted above all distinctions. How truly wonderful.

FURTHER STUDY

Acts 4:32–37;
2 Cor. 8:1–9

1. What characterised the life of the early Christians?

2. How does Paul encourage generosity?

Father, what a way to live – lifted above all distinctions. Do not let plenty entangle my spirit, nor poverty break it. No matter how I have lived in the past, this is how I long to live in the future. Please help me, my Father. Amen.

The generous eye

FOR READING & MEDITATION – 1 TIMOTHY 6:6–19

'Command them to do good, to be rich in good deeds, and to be generous and willing to share.' (v18)

Over the past few days we have been exploring steps we may need to take in becoming strong in relation to our finances. The friend whose steps we have been following said that these principles helped him to develop such spiritual strength and wisdom that he was confident he would never again be bound by money matters.

His final step was this: become a generous person. Look again at today's text. Woven through the fabric of the verses, as well as many others in the New Testament, is the thought: give, give, give. When you have money, don't be tempted to just hold it: release it. Let generosity become your trademark. This is not to say that you have to give all your money away, but give as much as you can, and as much as you believe God would have you give. Jesus once said, 'if your Eye is generous, the whole of your body will be illumined' (Matt. 6:22, Moffatt). What does this mean? If your eye – your outlook on life, your whole way of looking at things and people – is generous, then your whole personality is illumined; it is lit up.

FURTHER STUDY

Luke 21:1–4;
2 Cor. 9:6–11

1. For what did Jesus commend the widow?

2. How should we give and why?

Jesus was generous towards all, with all that He had to give, and this relates not just to money but also in His attitude toward the sick, the needy, the sinful and the unlovely. Whoever was before Him, His whole personality was full of light. Like Jesus – begin to look at everybody with a generous eye. Don't be mean spirited. Be generous, even to a fault. Better to err on the side of generosity than on the side of meanness. A friend of mine once said to me: 'Whenever I find myself in financial difficulties I start to give, give and give.' There is something in that idea, I believe.

Lord Jesus, help me this day and every day of my life from now on to make generosity the basis of all my dealings with people. Make me the channel and not the dead end of all Your generosity to me. For Your dear name's sake. Amen.

Coming back from failure

FOR READING & MEDITATION – ACTS 2:14–24

'Then Peter stood up with the Eleven, raised his voice and addressed the crowd' (v14)

Having looked at a number of places where life can break us, we move on now to consider the matter of personal failure. It may seem as if I am about to repeat what I said concerning shattered hopes and plans. But there is a difference. When discussing shattered hopes and plans we talked about something happening from without which caused our plans to be crushed, but here I have in mind those times when you thought you were equal to a task but for some reason you gave way within.

It is quite likely that someone reading this is caught up in a vortex of pessimism and gloom due to a recent, or even a not-so-recent, failure. You may be feeling like the man who once told me: 'I'm stunned by my failure. My stomach twists and turns. I'm so upset I cannot sleep. I've read that "the bird with the broken wing will never soar as high again". Does that mean I can never rise to the heights in God I used to know?'

We talked together of Simon Peter – a man with one of the worst track records in the New Testament. Peter was prejudiced, intolerant, stubborn and spiritually insensitive. Again and again he failed to get the point, for instance when he tried to prevent Christ from going to His death in Jerusalem (Matt. 16:22). On the eve of Christ's crucifixion, he no doubt felt he had failed when he denied Jesus with curses. I can imagine the devil whispering in his ear: 'Now you've really blown it; you're finished this time. A failure. You'll be forgotten, replaced.' But by God's grace, Peter rose from failure to success. He became strong at the broken places. Two of his letters have been recorded for ever in the Scriptures.

FURTHER STUDY

Matt. 16:13–20;
Luke 22:31–34;
John 21:15–19

1. What was Jesus' promise to Peter, and His prayer for him?

2. How did Jesus help Peter come back from failure?

Father, help me understand that no failure is a failure if it succeeds in driving me to Your side. All things serve me – when I serve You. I am so grateful. Amen.

Give a gift to help the nex

Help secure the future of CWR

So much of CWR's ministry is only possible because of the generosity, prayers and support of those who leave us gifts in their Will. Imagine the difference you could make through your legacy...

Be the reason a child gets to know Jesus
'Our daughter has been reading Topz for over a year now and we feel sure that God is using it to help her grow her faith.'

Help someone overcome anxiety, depression or grief with our Christian counselling training
'I feel more of God's love, and know that I have crossed a line from the past and am now moving to the future.'

Send life-changing biblical resources into prisons
'Daily readings are an important part of my faith here and I only wish I had read more in the past. God is truly blessing me with "freedom", despite being behind bars.'

eneration this Christmas

**Include a gift to CWR in your Will and enable us
to continue our ministry for generations to come.**

- Help people to apply God's Word to their
  daily lives
- Serve the Church with resources and teaching
- Equip counsellors to help people live their lives
  to the fullness God intended

*'Leaving a gift to CWR in our Will makes
sense! We believe in CWR's work and have the
opportunity to help. We have supported CWR for
years and want to continue to do so in the future.'*

The legacy gifts that supporters leave to CWR
enable us to respond to God's call to continue
serving His people. After you've taken care of
loved ones, would you consider leaving a gift to
CWR in your Will to help preserve and grow our
work for future generations?

Please get in touch if you have any questions,
or would like to know more about leaving a gift
to CWR in your Will.
Email **partners@cwr.org.uk**
or call **+44 (0)1252 784709**

Incisive questions

FOR READING & MEDITATION – ECCLESIASTES 7:21–29

'So I turned my mind to understand, to investigate and to search out wisdom and the scheme of things' (v25)

What are the steps we take when feeling crushed with failure, so that we can become strong at the place of weakness? As we think about this, please keep in mind that the principles I am suggesting are not only restorative, but also preventative.

The first thing we do whenever we have failed, is to explore the reason for the failure. These are some of the questions we might ask ourselves: have I contributed in any way to this issue by inattention to detail, lack of preparation, naivety, wrong timing, failure to weigh up the pros and cons, disregard of personal integrity, or insensitivity to other people's feelings? We might also ask: what does God want me to learn from this failure? It is extremely difficult, of course, to sit down and question yourself like this when failure floods in. But as the disappointments subside, as soon as possible after the event, try to work out what can be learned by honestly facing your emotions – emotions such as hurt, anger and anxiety. Remember, when you stop learning, you stop living.

FURTHER STUDY

Acts 2:37–41;
1 Tim. 1:15–17

1. What was the people's response to Peter's sermon?

2. What helped Paul face his failure?

If a failure occurs through no fault of your own, is God, I wonder, wanting to draw your attention to a purpose He may have for you that may take you in another direction? I have mentioned before how I failed a test to become an engine driver when I was eighteen. At that time I was simply crazy about steam engines, so when the news was conveyed to me, I was devastated. But if I had become an engine driver would I have wanted to become a preacher? I don't know, but my guess is probably 'No'. God was in that failure, I am perfectly sure.

Father, help me face my failures in the knowledge that some good can come from even the most difficult circumstances. Help me to be brave in my questions and to hear and receive Your perceptive, grace-filled answers. In Jesus' name. Amen.

'I didn't'

FOR READING & MEDITATION – HEBREWS 12:1–13

'Let us fix our eyes on Jesus... who for the joy set before him endured the cross' (v2)

Another thought to keep in mind when we collapse under the weight of failure is this: if the thing in which you failed was clearly the right thing for you to do, then dedicate your energies to God, try again, and don't give up.

A father who was attempting to encourage his teenage son after he had failed an exam said, 'Don't give up, try again.' 'What's the use?' responded the son. 'It's easier to quit.' His father challenged him, saying, 'The people who are remembered in life are the people who, when they failed, didn't give up, but tried again.' He went on, 'Remember Churchill? He didn't give up! Remember Thomas Edison? He didn't give up!' The boy nodded. His father continued, 'Remember John McCringle?' The boy was puzzled. 'Who's John McCringle?' he asked. 'You see,' said the father, 'you don't remember him – he gave up.'

I once saw a poster that impressed me deeply. It showed a man sitting on a park bench looking depressed and downcast. His arms were folded across his chest and he had a resigned look on his face. The caption read: 'I give up.' When I saw this poster, I looked at it for a few moments and turned away. But then I glanced at it again and my eye was attracted to something in the right-hand corner of the poster. It was a picture of a black hill and on it a very tiny cross. These words, barely perceptible, were printed beneath it: 'I didn't.'

Have you failed in something and, as a consequence, are feeling so discouraged that you don't even feel like trying again? Then lift your eyes to the cross. The one who triumphed over all obstacles holds out His hand towards you. Take His hand, and in His strength and power, try again.

FURTHER STUDY

Heb. 10:32–39;
2 Pet. 1:5–11

1. How important is perseverance?

2. What do we need to add to our faith?

God, help me to connect my smallness to Your greatness, my faint-heartedness to Your boldness, my fear to Your faithfulness. Then nothing can stop me. In that frame of mind, I will pick myself up and try again. Amen.

Grace – greater than failure

FOR READING & MEDITATION – 2 CORINTHIANS 9:6–15

'And God is able to make all grace abound to you' (v8)

Another amazing truth at hand when we fail is that God's grace continues to flow. You will no doubt have noticed that I am emphasising 'grace' a great deal in this issue. Where would we be without it? God does not stop being gracious just because we have blown something by our inability to prepare well or evaluate a situation in the right way. Grace is there not only when we confess our sins; it is also there when we have to confess to failure.

We can beat ourselves up more than we should when we fail, although we do need to own and face any possible self-inflicted issues. However, providing we respond correctly, God's grace will help us deal with it and enable us to get back on track once again. We know from Scripture that God can turn everything to good – even our failures.

FURTHER STUDY

Luke 19:1–10;
1 Tim. 1:12–14

1. How did Zacchaeus seek to be responsible?

2. How did the Lord deal with Paul's past?

There is one caution we should explore before leaving this point: we do not attempt to forget our failures if they have brought distress to others. Instead we should seek to act responsibly towards those we may have hurt.

When we face matters with honesty and integrity, then God transforms everything by His grace. He wipes away the burning memories of shame and the self-dislike, so that our failures, through His grace, do not paralyse us but propel us forward. You will have noticed, I am sure, that the Old Testament ends with a curse (Mal. 4:6), but the New Testament ends with grace (Rev. 22:21). Grace is the last word in everything. You are under grace today, and you will be under grace tomorrow. The past can't hurt you, and the future can't overcome you.

Father, I am so thankful that grace holds the keys of yesterday and tomorrow. You lock the one – and open the other. And there is grace for today too! I am eternally grateful. Amen.

The pressure's off

FOR READING & MEDITATION – 2 CORINTHIANS 1:12–22

'Now it is God who makes both us and you stand firm in Christ.' (v21)

For one more day we examine the principles and truths which can help us become strong at the place of failure. A further principle is this: strive not so much to succeed, but to do the right thing. While this is primarily preventative rather than corrective, if put into practice it may save us from unnecessary heartaches in the future.

On a visit to the USA, I addressed a group of ministers in Atlanta, Georgia, on the theme of 'Pitfalls in the Ministry'. I told them about my own failures, which amounted to a great many, and I said: 'The lesson I have learned from my failures is that I don't always have to succeed. I have to do the right thing under God's guidance, and leave success or failure in His hands.' One of the ministers quietly said to me afterwards: 'I'm regarded by my peers as one of the most successful ministers in my denomination. But today you have helped me overcome the greatest pressure in my life – the pressure to succeed.'

In the early years of my ministry I was very success-oriented; when I succeeded, I felt good, and when I failed, I felt devastated. Then God seemed to whisper to me in one of my prayer times, 'Are you willing to be a failure?' The question so shocked me that it was a whole week before I could answer that question with a 'Yes'. But when I did, I was instantly released from the two things that had crippled my life and ministry – the pressure to succeed and the fear of failure. From then on, what mattered to me was not succeeding or failing, but being true to Him. Success and failure are in His hands. I am not on the way to success, I am on the Way. There's a difference.

FURTHER STUDY

Luke 10:1–11; Rom. 15:14–19

1. How were the disciples free from the pressures of success or failure?

2. In what terms did Paul describe his ministry?

Father, set me free today from these two crippling evils – the pressure to succeed and the fear of failure. Help me to do the right thing and to leave success or failure in Your hands. For Jesus' sake. Amen.

The place to start

FOR READING & MEDITATION – PSALM 9:1–20

'For he who avenges blood remembers; he does not ignore the cry of the afflicted.' (v12)

It would be impossible to write on the theme of becoming strong at the broken places without mentioning the problem of unmerited suffering and distress. People say: 'My suffering is so great that I sometimes doubt the existence of a God of love. Can you tell me something that will help me regain my faith in this tragic hour?'

One of the most disturbing components of suffering is that there often seems to be no meaning in it – it seems so senseless, useless, leading nowhere. One writer has said that anyone who is undisturbed by the problem of unmerited suffering is a victim of either a hardened heart or a softened brain. He is right. Everyone who is alive, especially if he or she believes in a God of love, finds this problem difficult to resolve. No wonder the poet cried out:

FURTHER STUDY

Isa. 49:13–18;
James 5:10–11

1. Can God ever forget His people?

2. Of what is Job said to be an example?

My son, the world is dark with griefs and graves,
So dark that men cry out against the heavens.

I suppose there is nothing that makes people cry out against the heavens so much as the anguish that comes uninvited and is unmerited. I use the words 'uninvited' and 'unmerited' because some of our sufferings are the result of our own thoughtlessness or poor choices. But what about the times when life breaks us with sufferings and distress that are not directly related to our actions? Does God remember us then? Our text today says that He does. This in itself can help to keep us courageous, if not carefree; in peace, if not in happiness. Know this truth: God remembers you in your suffering. That may not be where we want to end but it is the place where we start.

Lord Jesus, You who experienced suffering in a way I will never know, hold me close to Your heart so that my sufferings will not diminish me but develop me. In Your precious name I pray. Amen.

Suffering is inevitable

FOR READING & MEDITATION – JOB 5:1–18

'Yet man is born to trouble as surely as sparks fly upward.' (v7)

Today we ask: how can we, as Christians, cope with the problem of unmerited suffering? What in life do we put in place or need to understand, if we are to become strong at this place where so many are broken? First, we recognise that all creation has been greatly disrupted by sin, and with it entered undeserved suffering.

What follows is something I read in an article by Dr E. Stanley Jones, a missionary to India. In an Indian palace, centuries ago, a child was born whose parents decided to keep all signs of decay and death from him. When he was taken into the garden, maids were sent before him to remove the decaying flowers and fallen leaves so that he would be protected from any indication of death. One day, however, he left his home and, while wandering through the streets, came across a corpse. His reaction was so strong that he set about establishing the teaching that, as life is fundamentally suffering, the only thing to do is to escape into Nirvana, the state of extinction of self. That young man was Gautama Buddha, whose beliefs are shared by millions of his followers, not only in India, but around the world. His philosophy is an extreme and dramatic result of trying to protect oneself from the realities of life, one of which is suffering.

FURTHER STUDY

1 Cor. 1:17–25;
Heb. 9:11–15

1. How important was the message of the cross to Paul?

2. What did the sufferings of Christ achieve?

The Christian faith is the opposite of that; it exposes us to the very heart of suffering – the cross. Jesus takes that suffering and turns it into salvation. We need not be afraid to face the fact that suffering may come our way, because we know that with God it can be redeemed. By that I mean He can work through suffering for a good and compassionate purpose.

Father, I am so thankful for the message of the cross. Whatever I may suffer, nothing can be compared to the suffering our Saviour endured there. Thank You, too, that You can bring good out of all things – even suffering. Amen.

The university of adversity

FOR READING & MEDITATION – JOB 2:1–10

'Shall we accept good from God, and not trouble?' (v10)

Today's text presents us with a great challenge. One commentator says it is 'the most profound verse in the Bible'. Can we accept suffering and distress as coming from God?

Christians are divided on this issue, and over the centuries the question has led to some heated arguments among God's people. Some say God is too good to send suffering to His people. All distress comes from the devil, they claim, and it should never be laid at God's door. Others say God never actually sends or wills affliction, but He does allow it to come so that He can work through it His good and perfect purposes. Those who picture God as a celestial being dropping nice little gifts from time to time into the laps of His children might struggle with the thought of Him as one who not only gives good gifts to His children, but allows troubles and adversity to come to them as well. If, however, God sees that adversity and suffering are the best means to achieve His purpose for us, then that is what He will allow or, depending on your view, send.

It is important, I believe, to see that in His relationships with His people, God is not obliged to make us comfortable. That is why it is unhelpful to tell those new to faith, 'Trust God, and your troubles will all be over.' That is unfair, confusing and frankly unbiblical. In fact, being a Christian may mean that you have more troubles than you had before your conversion. The difference is, however, that behind the troubles God allows (or sends), a divine purpose is being worked out. To have God with you in your troubles is better by far than to have a trouble-free existence and no sense of His divine presence.

FURTHER STUDY

2 Thess. 1:3–7;
1 Pet. 4:12–19

1. Why does Paul give thanks for the Thessalonians?

2. How are we to face suffering as Christians?

Father, if ever I needed Your help it is now. It's easy for me to accept good from Your hand – but adversity? Please help me come to terms with this challenging thought. In Jesus' name I ask it. Amen.

The agony of God

THURS
29 NOV

FOR READING & MEDITATION – ISAIAH 53:1–12

'Surely he took up our infirmities and carried our sorrows, yet we considered him stricken by God' (v4)

Yesterday we started to think about a matter that many might find difficult to understand – that troubles as well as good things may come to us from God. Today, therefore, I would like to unpack this a little further. It has been said that Christianity is the only religion that dares ask its followers to accept suffering as coming from God because it is the only religion that dares say God, too, has suffered.

Some might ask: just how much has God suffered? God's sufferings were not limited to the hours when He watched His Son being stripped and tortured and skewered to a cross. God's suffering started much further back in time. The Bible tells us that Christ was 'the Lamb that was slain from the creation of the world' (Rev. 13:8). That means that there was a cross set up in the heart of God long before there was a cross set up on the hill of Calvary. God's sufferings began before He laid the foundations of the world. The pain of the cross must have pierced Him as He awaited that awful moment when His Son would die on Calvary. How long did He wait? Centuries? Millennia! Then finally it came – the awful dereliction and agony of the crucifixion.

FURTHER STUDY

Acts 8:26–35;
Eph. 1:3–7;
1 Pet. 1:17–21

1. Who is the prophet Isaiah talking about?

2. With what have we been redeemed?

Was this the end of His suffering? No. Now His sufferings continue in the world's rejection of His Son, and in the indifference of some of His children. We should always remember that although living in this world is causing us pain, the pain God has suffered, and is suffering, is greater than anything we shall experience. Still, as the hymn says, 'Grace and love, like mighty rivers, pour incessant from above; and heaven's peace and perfect justice kiss a guilty world in love.'

Father, I realise that now I am thinking about the deepest mystery of the universe – Your sacrificial love. Help me to understand this more clearly, for when I see this, I see everything. Amen.

God is in control

FOR READING & MEDITATION – ISAIAH 46:3–13

'I say: My purpose will stand, and I will do all that I please.' (v10)

If there is one question to which there is no full and clear answer, it is the one asked by so many Christians: why does God allow His children to suffer? We can attempt to answer the question, like Job's 'comforters', but ultimately there are no clear and truly satisfying solutions.

It was a wonderful moment in my life when I was delivered from the torment of trying to figure out an answer to this question. I was looking at the passage in Isaiah, which is today's reading, when the thoughts I am about to share with you ran through my mind. God is in control of the world. He knows what He is doing. And a God who gave His Son to die for me on the cross has got to have an intelligent and compassionate purpose in whatever He does. Don't try to grasp all the ramifications of this truth; just accept it. From that moment on I hardly spent a single second trying to work out why God does what He does. I accepted His sovereignty without question – and was all the better spiritually for doing so.

'One of the marks of maturity,' comments Charles Swindoll, 'is the quiet confidence that God knows what He is doing, and a freedom from the pressure to understand why He does what He does.' The prophet Daniel said, 'He does according to his will in the host of heaven and among the inhabitants of the earth; and none can stay his hand or say to him, "What doest thou?"' (Dan. 4:35, RSV). So if you are always struggling to answer the question 'Why does God allow or send suffering and adversity?', I suggest you give up your struggle. You can't work things out anyway. Face the fact that God's ways are unsearchable. And He always knows best.

FURTHER STUDY

Isa. 40:25–31; 55:6–9; Rom. 11:33–36

1. What makes God incomparable?

2. Turn Paul's doxology into your own psalm of praise.

My gracious Father, set me free today from the tyranny of trying to fathom the unfathomable. Quietly I breathe the calm and peace of Your sovereignty into my being. No longer will I struggle to understand; I will just stand. Amen.

Un-Christian emotions

FOR READING & MEDITATION – MATTHEW 9:1–8

'Jesus... said to the paralytic, "Take heart, son; your sins are forgiven."' (v2)

Over the past month, we have looked at several areas of life where we can be broken and worn down, and we have seen that it is possible to be made strong at those broken places. Now we focus on the issue of continued ill health. Many reading these lines, myself included, are in the situation of finding that despite prayer and excellent medical attention, ill health continues. My testimony concerning this, as well as that of thousands of other Christians, is that God can make His people strong at even this place of brokenness. But how?

Well, before answering that question, we must first acknowledge that we can create our own ill health, both physically and emotionally. A Christian physician says: 'In the last century we have come to the realisation that worry, fear, anger and hatred are poisons that can cripple and destroy the body as well as the mind.' This doesn't mean that any and all of our particular physical problems, if we have any, are due to some inner resentment, but it is important to recognise that it may be so. In fact, doctors claim that 60–80% of our physical problems are psychosomatic – that is, triggered by a negative emotion. One doctor told me that many of the symptoms he sees in his office are 'the involuntary confessions of some internal guilt'.

When Jesus said to the paralysed man, 'Your sins are forgiven,' did He see a connection between his sense of guilt and his paralysis? I think so. Jesus lifted the guilt first and then the body was released from its bondage. Consider this as you go about your life today: ask God to help you identify anything that you may need to do to improve your health.

FURTHER STUDY

Psa. 31:9–16; Prov. 3:1–10

1. How did the psalmist recover his faith?

2. What kind of wisdom brings health?

My Father and my God, I see that I owe it to You and to myself to ensure all my emotions contribute to my health. Please help me to understand any unhealthy emotions I may be harbouring. In Jesus' name. Amen.

Attitudes affect our arteries

FOR READING & MEDITATION – PSALM 32:1–11

'Blessed is the man... in whose spirit is no deceit.' (v2)

Yesterday we ended by asking God to help us identify any thing we can do to improve our health. An American doctor, Charles T. Bingham claimed: 'Worry, fear and anger are the greatest disease causers. If we had perfect faith, we wouldn't worry about a thing.' The Japanese have a very interesting character in their language for disease; it means 'the spirit in trouble'.

For centuries physicians thought disease was the body in trouble and, as a result, operations have been performed for physical difficulties that really could not be resolved in that way. Then, in the twentieth century, doctors began to talk about psychosomatic problems – the recognition that some diseases are rooted in the *soma* (the Greek word for 'body') and some in the *psyche* (the Greek word for 'soul'). Doctors at the Mayo Clinic in the USA were reported as saying that they can deal with only 25% of the patients that come to them with the instruments of science; the remaining 75% need to change their attitudes before they can get well.

FURTHER STUDY

Psa. 39:1–7;
Prov. 4:20–27

1. What lesson has the psalmist learned?

2. How does Proverbs connect a healthy mind and body?

There is no doubt that Christian attitudes to life – forgiveness of others, generosity of spirit, and so on – would clear up a great many physical illnesses. I have learned, whenever I have fallen ill, to ask myself if any harboured wrong attitude has contributed to my state of health, and sometimes I have found it has. It is important to check up on our attitudes, for our attitudes can greatly affect our arteries. But what if we are broken by continued ill health which does not stem from the mind or the soul? Can God help us there? That is the issue with which we must come to grips in the next few days.

Father, I see that I must be healthy in mind and soul if I am to be healthy in body. Help me bombard every cell of my body with Christian attitudes and a positive mindset. In Jesus' name. Amen.

A wrong view of God

FOR READING & MEDITATION – JAMES 5:13–20

'Is any one of you sick? He should call the elders of the church to pray over him and anoint him with oil in the name of the Lord.' (v14)

How do we deal with the situation when we continue to struggle with ill health and are sure we are not harbouring ungodly attitudes? What do we do when we pray for healing, receive good medical attention, but still there is no release or even relief?

First, even though we may have already prayed for healing, it is right, I believe, to continue to do so and to invite other Christian friends, if possible, to join us in a prayerful pursuit of healing. Take today's text, which tells us that when we fall sick we call on the elders of the church and ask them to anoint us with oil. Christians hold different views regarding this text. Some say our first action when we become ill should be to call for the elders and not a medical doctor, whereas others advocate trying a medical remedy first and if that fails, to then call for the elders. Each person must decide what they wish to do. God heals directly, but He also heals through medicine.

We also need to remember that in James' day there were few medical doctors, and those that existed did not have the resources available today. My own feeling is that if an illness persists (especially after medical attention), I would advise, as a next step, to be anointed with oil. However, we need to be balanced and also recognise that God has put medical practitioners in the community to help us. If you go to a doctor first and not to the elders, don't then think that God will refuse to have anything to do with you. That is simply not true of God's character and what we read of Him in the Bible. If that is the way you think God acts, then you need to change your view of Him.

FURTHER STUDY

Psa. 103:1–5;
Luke 15:11–24

1. How does the psalmist celebrate salvation for the whole person?

2. What did the prodigal son discover about his father's heart?

God, forgive me if I hold within my heart a wrong image of You. Help me to remember that You have a Father's heart. You relate to me with love, care and understanding. In Jesus' name I pray. Amen.

Using even an illness

FOR READING & MEDITATION – GALATIANS 4:1–14

'As you know, it was because of an illness that I first preached the gospel to you.' (v13)

If there is one lesson I have learned – and it is one that I am most grateful for – it is that God can take what was meant for bad and turn it to good. A reader once wrote and suggested I should have those words put on my gravestone! When God doesn't heal a sickness is it because He is prevented from doing so? No, it is because He can use illness for a purpose that might not easily be seen by us.

In today's reading, Paul reminds the Galatians that it was because of an illness that he first preached the gospel to them. How I wish he had told us more about the circumstances. What kind of illness was it? Was it malaria? Was it an illness that affected his sight? (Some think his reference in verse 15 to the Galatians being willing to give him their eyes gives credence to this idea.) How long did the illness last? We do not know, of course, but what we do know is that the illness contributed to him raising up Christian churches there in Galatia, and then writing them a letter that has greatly enriched the ages.

In 1958 I had an illness which almost took my life, but it turned me from one direction in my ministry to another. The lessons I learned from that time prepared me for the writing of *Every Day with Jesus*. This ministry has become my major contribution to the Church and it has enabled me to reach more people than I ever could have done through the preached word. Though, as we said, we are told little about Paul's illness, we do know that it was used by God to spread His kingdom. God either heals in answer to prayer or He uses the illness to further His purposes – if we let Him. So either way, we win.

FURTHER STUDY

Psa. 105:16–24;
Jer. 32:17–27

1. What lesson does the psalmist recall in Joseph's life?

2. What did Jeremiah learn of God's possibilities?

Father, I am so glad that nothing can outsmart or outmanoeuvre You. You are always able to advance Your purposes. How thankful I am that I belong to a God who can turn everything to good. Amen.

Grace – in endless supply

FOR READING & MEDITATION – 2 CORINTHIANS 12:1–10

'for Christ's sake, I delight in weaknesses... For when I am weak, then I am strong.' (v10)

We must spend one more day on the question: when broken by continued ill health, can we be made strong at the broken places? I do not wish to be insensitive in what I am now about to say, because I know that some illnesses can be so upsetting that the ordeal can induce misery and chronic weariness. My own battle with prostate cancer brought me to moments of despondency. I do not pretend to be a warrior when it comes to ill health, but I am aware that in the deepest and darkest moments there is always a stream of strengthening and uplifting power that flows from God, and that this helps to comfort and sustain.

FURTHER STUDY

Psa. 25:12–22; Heb. 4:12–16

1. How does the psalmist respond to affliction?

2. How are we encouraged by knowing Jesus as our High Priest?

Non-Christians are often puzzled and intrigued by this quiet inner strength, which we commonly call 'grace'. But my own experience has proved to me that what I have taught and believed concerning the sustaining grace of God is indeed a glorious fact. I have felt a strength supporting me for which there can be no other explanation than that God is at work.

When Paul asked God three times to take away the 'thorn in his flesh' he was promised, not deliverance, but grace to use the affliction. We do not know what Paul's 'thorn in the flesh' was, but we do know there was enough grace available for him to endure it. When God does not take something away, even though you continue to plead with Him, He will give you a supply of grace that will enable you to cope with it. This is an issue of trusting in Him and being open to receive. When in need of grace, I picture myself standing under a waterfall and open every cell in my body to it. As soon as you open the doors of your being, I promise you God's grace will flow in.

Father, how thankful I am for the grace that can turn my weakness into strength. The only thing that can block it is my reluctance to open myself to it. Please teach me how to receive Your grace, my Father. In Jesus' name. Amen

Troublesome doubts

FOR READING & MEDITATION – JOHN 20:19–31
'Thomas said to him, "My Lord and my God!"' (v28)

Now we move on to consider another cause of Christians experiencing brokenness: deep and depressing doubts. All those who are entrusted with the care of souls – for example, pastors and counsellors – will have dealt with people who, after having received Christ as their Saviour, are lashed by devastating doubts. Some of these individuals go through a deep agony of the soul as they wrestle inwardly with this problem of doubt and can become spiritually exhausted.

I once met someone like this. She was a scientist and had serious doubts about certain parts of the Scriptures. 'I'm afraid that one day I'll wake up,' she said, 'and discover that science has disproved large chunks of the Bible.' I could sympathise with her, but in reality her doubts were quite unfounded. Science – real science, that is – will never disprove the Bible. Half-baked science may appear to discredit the truth of God's Word, but real science only ever validates it.

The classic example of a person who doubted is the disciple Thomas. We call him 'doubting Thomas', but that is largely an unfair label. How sad it is that often we pick out a negative trait in a person and label them according to that one thing. Thomas had his moment of doubt, but he became strong at the broken place. How strong? Let history judge. A well-authenticated tradition has it that Thomas went to India and founded a strong church there. Even today there are Christians in India who call themselves by his name – the St Thomas Christians. They are some of the finest Christians I have ever met. Thomas had his doubts allayed in one glorious moment of illumination – and then he went places. So can you!

FURTHER STUDY

Mark 9:17–24;
Rom. 4:16–25

1. How does Jesus rescue us from an 'unbelieving generation'?

2. How did Abraham overcome his doubts?

My Father, just as You took Thomas and changed him from a doubter to a man of amazing faith and achievement, so I pray that You will do the same for me. For Your own dear name's sake I ask it. Amen.

Truth in the inner parts

FOR READING & MEDITATION – PSALM 51:1–19

'Surely you desire truth in the inner parts' (v6)

W hat should we do when we find ourselves harassed by honest doubts? Well, first we learn to distinguish between honest doubts and defensive doubts. A number of doubts that trouble people concerning the Christian faith are attempts, made half-consciously, I believe, to hide some moral issue or failure. I am not denying that some people experience acute intellectual problems in relation to their faith, and it would be wrong to suggest, or even hint, that everyone troubled by doubts is consciously or unconsciously using them as a smoke screen. But because experience has shown that some do, this issue has to be faced.

So, difficult though it may be, ask yourself now: am I using my doubts as a 'defence mechanism' to cover up some struggle or personal choice issue? Adam used a defence mechanism when he blamed Eve for his sin. This type of defence mechanism is called projection – refusing to face up to personal responsibility and projecting the blame onto someone else. Could it be that some of your doubts may be due to this? If you are willing to look at this issue objectively, or perhaps with the help of a wise and responsible Christian friend, then that would be a good move. Reflect on the words of an ancient hymn:

FURTHER STUDY

Jer. 17:9–14;
Luke 5:1–11

1. Why was Jeremiah's self-distrust healthy?

2. What truth did Peter face up to?

> *Jesus, the hindrance show,*
> *Which I have feared to see,*
> *Yet let me now consent to know*
> *What keeps me out of Thee.*

God never rejects this kind of plea.

Gracious Father, You know how difficult it is for me to see myself as I really am. Help me to be honest with myself – ruthlessly honest – for I long to be as honest as You. Please help me in this hour of challenge. In Jesus' name. Amen.

John's doubts about Jesus

FOR READING & MEDITATION – MATTHEW 11:1–11

'Are you the one who was to come, or should we expect someone else?' (v3)

An important thing to remember concerning this issue of doubt is that, although God would prefer us to believe, He is exceedingly loving and gracious towards those who struggle with genuine doubts. Did you notice when we were looking at Thomas two days ago that Jesus did not denounce his attitude of doubt, nor did He refuse his request for physical evidence that He truly was the Christ? Instead Jesus said to him: 'Put your finger here; see my hands. Reach out your hand and put it into my side. Stop doubting and believe' (John 20:27).

FURTHER STUDY

John 6:14–21; 10:40–42

1. How does Jesus deal with our fear?

2. What was John the Baptist's legacy?

The passage before us today tells of another occasion when a person closely associated with Jesus became oppressed by doubt. John the Baptist was in prison, and probably suffering great discomfort and disillusionment. From prison he sent some messengers to Jesus to ask if He really was the Messiah or if they should be looking for somebody else. John, you remember, had baptised Jesus, and had introduced Him to the world with these words: 'Look, the Lamb of God, who takes away the sin of the world' (John 1:29).

Does it not seem strange that John, who had witnessed the descent of the Holy Spirit upon Jesus at His baptism, should have developed doubts about who He was and the validity of His mission? How did Jesus respond to this situation? With tenderness and sensitivity. He said: 'Go back and report to John what you hear and see: The blind receive sight, the lame walk, those who have leprosy are cured, the deaf hear' (vv4–5). Jesus could have rebuked John, His doubting cousin, with strong words of reproof, but He didn't. Although Jesus is concerned when we have problems, He is more concerned about people.

Thank You, Father, for reminding me that You see me not as a problem but as a person. I know You are concerned about my doubts, but You are more concerned about me. I am deeply grateful. Amen.

Empower your church
to care

Many people face life challenges such as stress, job loss, illness, relationship difficulties or bereavement. **Paraclesis: Journeying Together** enables every person to take their own experiences and turn them into a gift of support and care for others around them. Scripture shows that God's heart is to see His children love and come alongside one another, just as He comes alongside us.

· Unlock the gift of life experience in your church
· Engage with the six-step initiative for pastoral care
· Strengthen your church's culture of care
· Recognise the value of the gift of journey in your church
· Release the hidden potential in your congregation

To help introduce **Paraclesis: Journeying Together** to your church, we have put together a free Introduction Pack which you can receive by signing up at **www.paraclesis.org.uk**

paraclesis
Coming alongside others

The muscles of faith

FOR READING & MEDITATION – JAMES 1:5–8

'But when he asks, he must believe and not doubt' (v6)

When dealing with honest doubts, another important principle to employ is this: make a conscious decision to doubt your doubts and believe your beliefs. One of the key issues of the Christian life, as we have been seeing, depends on how prepared we are to exercise our wills in favour of God and His Word. To do this, of course, requires faith – faith in the fact that God has revealed Himself in His Son and through the Scriptures.

FURTHER STUDY

Psa. 19:7–11;
119:9–16;
Rom. 10:10–17

1. What is the psalmist's attitude to God's Word?

2. How does faith come?

As a teenager, I had many doubts about the Scriptures. But one night I made a conscious decision to accept them as the eternal and inerrant Word of God. Please notice I said 'a conscious decision'. In other words, I decided by an action of my will to doubt my doubts and believe my beliefs. Then I discovered an astonishing thing. Both doubt and faith are like muscles – the more you flex them, the stronger they become. Up until that time I had been using the muscles of doubt to a great degree, but unfortunately I had failed to exercise the muscles of faith. When I made up my mind to accept the truth of God's Word by faith, muscles I never thought I had began to function. Now, many decades later, those muscles have developed to such a degree that I find it is easier to believe God than to doubt Him. I trace the beginnings of my spiritual development to that day, long ago, when I decided to take what one theologian terms 'the leap of faith'.

Perhaps today might become a similar day of decision for you. In this issue of *Every Day with Jesus* I have asked you to make decisions about many things – make one more today. Decide to doubt your doubts and believe your beliefs.

God, help me to know and trust You more. If I have been using the muscles of doubt more than the muscles of faith, then, from today, things will be different. I decide to take You and Your Word on trust. Amen.

Thomas, the doer

FOR READING & MEDITATION – ACTS 1:1–11

'But you will receive power when the Holy Spirit comes on you; and you will be my witnesses' (v8)

We spend one last day exploring some of the insights which enable us to overcome doubt and develop our faith. The final principle is this: recognise that if you did not doubt, you could not believe. So don't be intimidated by your doubts. The Christian writer Robert Brown said this: 'You call for faith: I show you doubt, to prove that faith exists. The more of doubt, the stronger faith, I say, if faith o'ercomes doubt.' Those who doubt most, and yet strive to overcome their doubts, become some of Jesus' most remarkable followers.

We began this section by looking at Thomas the doubter and we end by looking at Thomas the doer. One commentator says that Thomas, being a twin (his name 'Didymus' means 'twin', John 11:16), must have developed an early independence of judgment that made it possible for him to break with his twin and follow Jesus. This is an assumption, but I think it is a valid one. Perhaps it was that independence that led him to reject the testimony of the other disciples when they said, 'We have seen the Lord!' (John 20:25). When Jesus said to him, 'Reach out your hand and put it into my side. Stop doubting and believe' (John 20:27), his doubts vanished, and he responded, 'My Lord and my God!' (John 20:28).

Until then, no one had called Jesus 'God'. They had called Him 'Messiah', 'Son of God', 'Son of the living God' – but not 'God'. Here, Thomas the doubter leapt beyond the others and was the first to confess Jesus as God. And Thomas' faith did not stop there. As we said earlier, he almost certainly took the gospel to India. The doubter became a doer!

FURTHER STUDY

Acts 26:12–19; Gal. 1:11–24

1. How does Paul describe his life-changing encounter with Jesus?

2. How did Paul come to preach the faith rather than destroy it?

God, what a prospect – my faith, often so tentative, can, through Your illumination and my response, become an energising strength. It can not only save me, but also send me. May there be no limits! Amen.

In the heat of temptation

FOR READING & MEDITATION – 1 CORINTHIANS 10:1-13

'And God is faithful; he will not let you be tempted beyond what you can bear.' (v13)

Another reason why Christians are sometimes broken is because of relentless temptations. Perhaps at this very moment you are surrounded by a host of powerful temptations that threaten to overtake you. But take heart! Today's text assures us that God is committed to giving us the strength to face and overcome even the most appealing temptations.

Notice what the text is telling us: God has promised this and will do what He says. God is always true to His Word, His character and His love to support you in any situation that threatens to overwhelm you. He understands that you can do nothing without Him, and that you will certainly fail if He steps away. If God were to remove Himself from you in the critical moments when you are caught up in temptation, then He would not be true to Himself. Remember this: 'God is faithful; he will not let you be tempted beyond what you can bear.' God has promised this and will do what He says. Or, to put it another way, you will find an overflowing supply of grace when you are in the midst of the strong pull of temptation.

The faithfulness of God's promise does not necessarily consist of delivering us from the place of temptation, but in never allowing the temptation to be greater than our power to resist. God knows far better than we do just how much strength we have, and in the most amazing way, when we ask, He enables us to keep on track with Him. God will never permit temptations with more pull than we have strength to resist. He will increase the power of His assistance according to the strength of the temptation.

FURTHER STUDY

1 Cor. 1:1-9;
2 Thess. 3:1-5

1. What gave Paul confidence for the Corinthians' future?

2. How did Paul commend the Thessalonians to God?

Father, I am so thankful that I am not alone in this battle against temptation. Help me remember this and hold on to it no matter how fierce the temptation may be. In Jesus' name. Amen.

Unbeatable and unbreakable

FOR READING & MEDITATION – ISAIAH 54:11–17

'no weapon forged against you will prevail' (v17)

We continue considering the matter of how God can help us when we are feeling overwhelmed by temptations. Yesterday we began to understand that God is committed to strengthening us to face every temptation that comes our way, and that He has promised He will not permit one temptation to come to us that we cannot handle.

Temptation, though we may not think so when we face it, has possibly a greater purpose. As we grapple, we grow. Goethe said, 'Difficulties prove men.' They do. We can learn to do more with temptation than just bear it – we can learn to use it. Knowing how to face temptation and turn it to our advantage is one of life's greatest strengths. When we have learned it we are unbeatable and unbreakable.

A Christian schoolteacher once told me that when she was talking to her class about the cross, a little girl raised her hand and said, 'Jesus didn't just carry His cross – He used it'. 'From the lips of children and infants…' (Matt. 21:16)! God doesn't want us to just bear the cross of temptation; He wants us to use it. You can't bear a cross for long unless you use it. A stoic bears a cross; a Christian uses it and it bears him. Today, let's make a decision before we go any further: are we simply going to bear temptation or are we going to use it?

When we view temptation with the right attitude and face it with the strength and grace that God provides, then the things that oppose us contribute to our advancement. I once heard the singer Sammy Davis Jr take some words that were shouted to him from the audience and set them to music. It's not what comes that matters, it's what you do with it that counts.

FURTHER STUDY

1 Thess. 3:1–10; Heb. 2:11–18

1. Why did Paul rejoice over the Thessalonians?

2. How does Jesus help us overcome temptation?

Father, I see so clearly that when I am in You, and You are in me, then everything can be used – even temptation. Your grace enables me to be unbeatable and unbreakable. I am so thankful. Amen.

'It hurts good'

'Consider it pure joy... whenever you face trials... the testing of your faith develops perseverance.' (vv2–3)

At present we are saying that when we face temptation, God supplies us with sufficient grace to make the temptation not a groaning point but a growing point. Everything – temptation included – can be used for higher ends with the help of God. That is why as Christians we should not be too surprised, for everything can be made to work towards favourable ends. A soldier in the Iraq war was asked by a TV reporter: 'But isn't the weather unfavourable?' He replied, 'Weather in war is always favourable – providing you know how to use it.' That is the point we are making – everything can contribute if you know how to use it.

FURTHER STUDY

Luke 4:1–12;
2 Pet. 2:4–9

1. How did Jesus overcome temptation?

2. Whom does the Lord protect and rescue?

Philosophers have told us repeatedly that life is determined to a far greater extent by our reactions than by our actions. Temptation sweeps in upon us and forces its way into our lives without our asking (and oftentimes without our acting), and it is then that our reaction plays a vital part. We can react in self-pity and frustration or we can act with confidence and with courage and make the circumstances work to shape our character and deepen our hold upon God. That's what I mean by using temptation – using it to increase our dependence upon God and to draw closer to Him. Temptation has disrupting and damaging intentions, but resisting it brings spiritual growth.

I read that South American Indians like bitter medicine. They don't consider it beneficial unless it has an acrid taste. 'It hurts good,' they say. You can make temptation 'hurt good' when you see it as increasing your dependence upon God and developing your character, causing us to walk in a closer, daily, minute by minute relationship with Jesus.

Saviour, You who faced the bitterness of temptation and resisted in the strength of the Spirit, grant that I, too, might overcome. May I turn every temptation into a triumph. For Your own dear name's sake. Amen.

In the dark?

FOR READING & MEDITATION – JAMES 1:9–20

'Blessed is the man who perseveres under trial' (v12)

Today we ask: why does God allow temptation? In order to answer that, let's look at the Greek word for temptation used in the New Testament: *peirasmos*. It means to test, to try or to prove. The biblical use of the word (unlike the modern use of it) does not contain the idea of seduction or entrapment, but rather conveys the idea of testing or stretching a person to deepen their personal qualities. The reason God allows temptation, then, is because it can develop our character.

One writer comments, 'The conversion of a soul is the work of a moment, but the making of a saint is the work of a lifetime.' Oswald Chambers expressed the same truth differently: 'God can, in one single moment, make a heart pure, but not even God can give a person character.' Character would not be the precious thing it is if it could be acquired without effort. 'Virtue that has not been tried and tested,' said another great theologian, 'is not worthy of the name of virtue.'

It is essential, in a world such as this, that temptation comes to try the people of God, for without temptation there can be no advancement, no development, no growth in character. You may ask: what is character? It has been said that character is who we are in the dark. Reputation is what other people think of us; character is what we are on the inside. Character is the strength and refinement of soul that we develop as we stand against the tide of trials and temptation. We must have something to pit ourselves against if we are to develop in every area of life. As I said two days ago, as we grapple, we grow. And out of the growing comes character.

FURTHER STUDY

Rom. 5:1–5;
Heb. 10:32–39

1. What produces Christian character?

2. What are the positive results of enduring trials?

Father, if character is something achieved rather than acquired, then help me in the achieving. And if You allow temptation and trials in order to deepen my character, then I welcome them – in Your name. Amen.

Why fear temptation?

FOR READING & MEDITATION – 1 PETER 1:1–9

'These have come so that your faith… may be proved genuine' (v7)

For many people, the idea of God allowing His children to be tempted is inconsistent with His omnipotence. 'If God is almighty,' they reason, 'then He should intervene in any attempts to seduce us and prevent any undue influences on our personalities.' However, it is because God is omnipotent that He permits us to be tempted. After all, He allowed foreign nations to test Israel to see if they would keep His way (Judg. 2:22).

F.P. Harton says: 'A conquering nation that is not sure of its own strength refuses to allow the people it subjects any kind of independence at all, and keeps control with a strong hand.' God does not control His universe through fear but through eternal love and justice. Although He allows men and women to be tempted for the express purpose of building character, He ensures that to each one there flows a stream of divine empowerment, strength and grace that, when received, enables us to overcome temptations and use it to higher ends.

FURTHER STUDY

Gen. 39:6–10;
Heb. 12:4–12

1. How did Joseph overcome temptation?

2. What produces holiness and righteousness in us?

One of the devil's strategies is to attempt to persuade us that God is not able to help us in our time of temptation. God is indeed able to help us, and He helps, not by extracting us from the temptation, but by preserving us in the midst of it. If temptation is something God allows to happen here on earth, why fear it? However, it would be potentially dangerous and unwise to seek out temptation in order to prove we can overcome it – that would be presuming on our own strength. But because we know God can use it to develop our character, we need not fear it or be surprised when it comes. We may struggle in temptation, but out of the struggling can come a greater dependence on God.

Father, I see that though You do not send temptation, You do not insulate us from it either. Your strategy is to be with us in it and turn it to the development of our soul and spirit. I am so thankful. Amen.

Alone – yet not lonely

FOR READING & MEDITATION – JOHN 14:15–27

'I will not leave you as orphans; I will come to you.' (v18)

Afurther area where life can break us is the area of loneliness. The good news of the Christian faith is that this, too, can be turned from a struggle into a strength. We begin by understanding and unpacking the difference between loneliness and aloneness. It is possible to be alone and yet not lonely. Loneliness can be devastating and difficult to live through, partly because of our in-built need to connect with others, and it often includes feelings of depression, worthlessness and inner emptiness.

FURTHER STUDY

Jer. 15:16–21;
Heb. 13:1–8

1. How did the Lord console His lonely prophet?

2. How does Hebrews address our sense of isolation?

I have often referred to a story about the poet Rupert Brooke who died in World War I. When he sailed from Liverpool to New York on the *SS Cedrick*, he felt terribly lonely for there was no one to see him off. As he looked down from the ship he saw a scruffy little boy on the dockside and offered him some money if he would wave him off. The boy agreed and Brooke later wrote in his diary: 'I got my money's worth and my farewell – dear, dear boy.' Those who have never felt lonely may not understand a story like that, but to others it carries a whole world of meaning.

God's strength is able to reach us when we feel worn down and worthless due to loneliness. Our inner being can be flooded with such a consciousness of the divine presence that, even though we may still ache for a human companion, our heart will be warmed. Although we are alone, we will not feel devastatingly lonely. To some, this may sound far-fetched and not in keeping with reality. I speak, however, from experience. And what God has done for me, He can do also for you.

Father, I know in theory that when I have You I need never feel lonely, but please may this truth take hold of my heart as well as my head. For Jesus' sake. Amen.

No one as lonely as He

FOR READING & MEDITATION – MATTHEW 26:36–56

'Then all the disciples deserted [Jesus] and fled.' (v56)

Yesterday we made the comment that there is a difference between loneliness and aloneness. It is possible, we said, to be alone and yet not lonely. Loneliness is a feeling of being bereft, companionless, isolated. It can be quite devastating to feel lonely. Nor is that feeling of loneliness necessarily diminished when we are in the heart of a crowd or, for that matter, in a Christian church. Some churches have been described as places where lonely people go so that everyone might be lonely together. We can be in a crowd and not feel part of it.

Did Jesus ever feel lonely? I am sure He did. There were times, I imagine, especially as He drew near to the crucifixion, when He would have felt bereft of human companionship. The disciples were unable to enter into His feelings as He agonised in His soul about His impending suffering on Calvary. On the eve of His death, they argued about precedence, they slept while He wrestled in prayer in the Garden of Gethsemane, and when He was arrested, they ran away.

Most who have been willing to die for a cause have had the comfort of knowing that there were those who sympathised with them and understood the cause for which they were prepared to die. But even this eluded Jesus. His sacrifice mystified the people who were His closest companions. Not one single soul understood why He allowed Himself to be taken to the cross. This is why, whenever you feel lonely, you have the assurance that Jesus understands how you feel. He knew loneliness as no one has ever known it. And because He has felt as you feel, He is able to comfort you with an understanding that no one else can offer.

FURTHER STUDY

Psa. 27:7–14; 2 Cor. 4:7–14

1. How is the psalmist comforted in his loneliness?

2. What is the secret of Paul's resilience?

Lord Jesus, I see that no one has ever touched the same depths of loneliness as You. Please draw close to me in those moments when I feel lonely, and build my spiritual life so that You might use even this for Your glory. Amen.

'A trifle to talk about'

FOR READING & MEDITATION – MATTHEW 28:16–20

'And surely I am with you always, to the very end of the age.' (v20)

From experience, I know it is very difficult convincing those feeling crushed under the weight of loneliness that the lonelier you feel, the closer Jesus will come: but nevertheless, it is true. F.W. Robertson, a famous preacher of a past generation, was bitterly attacked by other Christians for the views he held, and as he approached the end of his life, his friends became fewer and fewer. It was in one of these dark periods, when it seemed that all his friends had left him, that he wrote: 'I am alone, lonelier than ever, sympathised with by none, because I sympathise too much with all, but the Almighty sympathises with me... I turn from everything to Christ. I get glimpses into His mind, and I am sure that I love Him more and more. A sublime feeling of His presence comes about me at times which makes inward solitariness a trifle to talk about.' Consider that last sentence again: 'A sublime feeling of His presence comes about me... which makes inward solitariness a trifle to talk about.' What a glorious testimony!

FURTHER STUDY

Psa. 16:1–11;
Acts 18:5–11

1. How is the psalmist strengthened by God's presence?

2. How did the Lord strengthen Paul?

Was this preacher just one of the favoured few who can feel like this? No, God has no favourites. With the assurance of the presence of Jesus promised to us all, none of God's people need feel the full weight of loneliness. Jesus walked that way so that no man or woman might walk it again. Not the elderly struggling to eke out an existence, neither married, nor widow, nor single parent – indeed, no single person – need feel the desolation of desertion. God will live closely with His children in any circumstances and give them such an inward strength that it will make 'inward solitariness a trifle to talk about'.

Father, what a promise! The lonelier I feel, the closer You come to me. Show me how to lay down all my barriers so that Your presence can come in and make this truth a reality in my life. For Jesus' sake. Amen.

FOR READING & MEDITATION – ROMANS 12:1–21

'Share with God's people who are in need. Practise hospitality.' (v13)

The subject of loneliness cannot be properly discussed without exploring the uncomfortable thought that some people bring loneliness upon themselves. Although the purpose of these studies is to focus on situations in which we find ourselves through little or no fault of our own, it would be helpful to pause and consider the fact that some forms of loneliness may be self-generated.

Those whose circumstances compel them to live alone need to learn to resist becoming inward-looking. Underlying attitudes can reinforce even the slightest feelings of loneliness, and potentially drive others away. 'In a needy world like ours,' said Dr W.E. Sangster, 'anybody can have friendship who will give it.' Ralph Waldo Emerson commented, 'The only way to have a friend is to be a friend.' And millions had discovered this long before Emerson made his observation. When a person says, 'I have no friends,' it practically invites the reponse, 'Have you been a friend?'

The Greek word *charis*, usually translated in the New Testament as 'grace', also means 'charm'. God's grace flowing into our lives can, both cheer the heart and add charm to our personalities. Have you noticed how two people in love become radiant? They not only become loving to each other, but their love spills over to others as well. This is what happens as God transforms us from the inside out; so let God's love flow into your life until it irradiates your human nature and fills you with His charm and attractiveness. Jesus' presence in your heart will help you to be a friend, and by being a friend you will find that friends are drawn to you.

FURTHER STUDY

Prov. 16:28; 17:9,17; 18:24; 27:6–10; 1 John 3:10–18

1. Define friendship, according to Proverbs.

2. If God so loves us, how should we respond?

Father, I needed this challenging word. If I have contributed to feeling lonely, help me to see this and to change my outlook. Fill me so full of Your love that it will illuminate my life. For Jesus' sake. Amen.

'I live in God'

FOR READING & MEDITATION – ACTS 17:22–34

'For in him we live and move and have our being.' (v28)

For one more day we consider the issue of loneliness. Many, we have said, are crushed by loneliness, but the question we are facing is this: can God turn even this into a strength? Clark Moustakas, a psychologist, claims we can look for the good in loneliness, for it can bring deeper perception, greater sensitivity and increased insight.

As you will no doubt have realised, one thing I continually emphasise is that everything can be used. I am not saying that we should regard loneliness as something wonderful, because that would be wrong. Loneliness can be painful, hurtful and sometimes almost unbearable. But if we recognise that God allows only what He can use, then instead of focusing on the problem we will begin to focus on how He can turn the situation to good. Those who have experienced the bitter depths of loneliness do indeed have a greater sensitivity to the hurts of others. Some of the most powerful prayer warriors I have known have been people who allowed God to take their pain and then started to intercede for others.

FURTHER STUDY

Psa. 17:6–15;
Jude 20–25

1. What images of God's grace strengthened the psalmist?

2. Reflect on the wonder of abiding in God's love.

One man I heard about who had known extreme loneliness but had opened up his heart to a deeper experience of God, went to live in a home for elderly people. A Christian friend who visited him said, 'I'm so sorry to see you living in this old people's home.' The elderly man drew himself up to his full height, and with a measured tone and dignity befitting the occasion responded, 'My friend, I do not live in this old folks' home; I live in God.' This is both challenging and exciting! Can we learn to live in God whatever our circumstances and situation? Let's ask this of God today.

Father, give me such a consciousness of Your presence that I shall never again feel lonely. Help me to open my heart to the grace that is flowing right now so that today I will know, truly know, how to live in You. In Jesus' name I pray. Amen.

Home – a dangerous place?

FOR READING & MEDITATION – JAMES 3:13–18

*'But the wisdom that comes from heaven is first of all pure;
then peace-loving' (v.17)*

Yet another cause of people experiencing brokenness is difficulties at home. It may be a marriage on the point of breaking up (or that has already broken up) or possibly an estrangement with one's children or parents. Or perhaps endless rows in the family that threaten to dampen the hopeful expectations of Christmas.

It has not escaped the notice of those who prepare statistics that there are more family breakdowns (and acts of self-harm) at Christmas than at any other time of the year. The reason for this, it seems, is that everyone is under pressure at Christmas to be happy. This expectation is often more than people can cope with, and as a result tempers fray. Sometimes the fall-out can fracture a home. Of all the matters we have thought about, none, perhaps, is as painful and traumatic as domestic difficulties.

FURTHER STUDY

Luke 1:15–17;
1 Pet. 3:7–12

1. What constitutes 'a people prepared for the Lord'?

2. How does the gospel transform relationships?

There are many more things that can cause trouble in the home: incompatibility, insensitivity, continued quarrels and disagreements, nagging, overuse of alcohol, irritating habits, emotional and physical violence, child neglect, difficulties with children, or an elderly family member who needs constant care and attention. A study conducted some years ago by an American university concluded that one of the most dangerous places to be – apart from a war zone or in a riot – is in the home.

The ultimate answer to domestic peace and happiness in the home is found in a homeless unmarried man whose power enables men and women to live the way they were designed. His power was never more needed than at this hour in our history.

Lord Jesus Christ, You who provide men and women with strength in the very place they need it, help us to live peaceably in the home as is Your original design. For Your own dear name's sake. Amen.

Needed in every home

FOR READING & MEDITATION – MARK 9:42–50

'Have salt in yourselves, and be at peace with each other.' (v50)

There can be little doubt that the family is being assailed from many directions. How sad that in an age when millions of houses are being built, at the same time thousands of homes are being broken. A well-known marriage guidance counsellor claims that half the troubles in the home could be overcome if all concerned understood the power of a simple apology. An apology often saves a situation. Someone has said:

An apology is a friendship preserver,
is often a debt of honour,
is never a sign of weakness,
is an antidote for hatred,
costs nothing but one's pride,
always saves more than it costs
and is a device needed in every home.

FURTHER STUDY

Psa. 34:8–14;
Col. 4:2–6

1. How does a 'taste' for God change things?

2. How may our speech 'taste' good?

In today's text Jesus says, 'Have salt in yourselves'. In other words, don't be dependent on your environment for life's taste. Draw from the life of God within you, and then in the rollercoaster of family life it will mean that you remain steady and are not going up and down emotionally.

In my view, one of the greatest causes of breaking peace with others is the sense of tastelessness within ourselves. We feel out of sorts with others because we are out of sorts with ourselves. A Christian who keeps in daily touch with God through prayer and the reading of His Word will be held together by the truth that life has inward taste, no matter what happens on the outside. Inward salt makes for outward peace.

Father, may I always have enough salt within myself as a result of my daily contact with You: to hold the home together, and in all other situations as well. In Jesus' name I ask it. Amen.

Next Issue

JAN/FEB 2019

Hold the Line

Are some of the key truths of our faith disappearing from Christian teaching today? Why is it less common nowadays to hear teaching on subjects such as the impact of sin, the authority of the Bible and the judgment of God?

Next issue, we explore some challenging areas of our faith, and rediscover some key principles for holiness so that we may firmly but graciously stand our ground and steadfastly cling to what we know to be truth.

Every Day
with Jesus

JAN/FEB 2019

Hold the Line

'Stand at the crossroads and look; ask for the ancient paths, ask where the good way is, and walk in it'
Jeremiah 6:16

Living life with Jesus. Every day

CWR

Also available as an
eBook/eSubscription

Obtain your copy from CWR, a Christian bookshop or your National Distributor.
If you would like to take out a subscription, see the order form at the back of these notes.

Your soul's security

FOR READING & MEDITATION – ACTS 1:12–26

'They all joined together... along with... Mary the mother of Jesus, and with his brothers.' (v14)

Three days ago we said that the ultimate answer to domestic peace and happiness is found in a homeless unmarried man whose power enables men and women to live the way they ought. Did you know that Jesus finally won His whole family to His cause? There was a time when 'his own brothers did not believe in him' (John 7:5), but just before Pentecost, as we see from today's reading, they were all gathered together to pray. Apparently they had all become part of the Church. What was it, I wonder, that won them to His cause? Well, I imagine His resurrection from the dead would have finally convinced them that He was who He claimed to be. But I am sure too that they were influenced by the relationship they saw He had with His heavenly Father.

FURTHER STUDY

Luke 1:45–55; Col. 3:9–17

1. How did Mary establish a God-exalting home for Jesus?

2. Make Paul's words a Christmas prayer for your family and friends.

Relationship with God is the key to holding strong and steady amid the flux of domestic difficulties. We must never elevate anyone – husband, wife or child – to the position where they become 'God' to us. If we depend on their appreciation, understanding, co-operation, and so on to hold us together, then when they let us down we will feel devastated. No one must take the place of God in our lives – no one.

I have found that the biggest single problem in relationships, whether in or outside the home, occurs when we try to get others to meet the deep needs of our soul, rather than God. When this happens we are extremely vulnerable to others' likes or dislikes. We can find ourselves manipulating them to be there for us, rather than focusing on how we can be there for them. When our dependence is first and foremost on God then, if others let us down, we may be hurt but we will not be destroyed.

Father, if I can get hold of this truth – really get hold of it – I see it can hold me fast when all things are breaking up around me. Help me to make You my soul's security – and You alone. In Jesus' name. Amen.

Do not be afraid

FOR READING & MEDITATION – MATTHEW 18:1–9

'And whoever welcomes a little child like this in my name welcomes me.' (v5)

Family life can be testing at times, especially in the build-up to Christmas, when anticipation and expectations are running high. Please let me be clear: there is no such thing as a perfect family. Family life can be wonderful, supportive, exhilarating – a real rollercoaster of emotions, allowing us to experience love and acceptance, and a tremendous sense of belonging – but it's also true that it can be difficult and painful, often all at the same time!

It's within our families that we first begin to learn how to extend and receive love, forgiveness and graciousness; how to live out authentic relationships 'up close and personal'. We learn a great deal (albeit unconsciously) from our parents, carers and those who share our homes. You may have heard it said that the best thing parents can do for their children is to love each other. A home or family in which we see and experience God-infused love and acceptance is very powerful, and it leaves no one unaffected.

It's in our family and close relationships that we are often most sensitive and vulnerable; where we will often experience the greatest joy, and also possibly the greatest pain. If your family and home life has been difficult or even disastrous, I encourage you this Christmas Eve to pause. Consider with me now, the angels on the hillside who, no longer able to contain themselves, broke out into glorious light, piercing the dark night sky, announcing to the shepherds God's hope for the world. Such good news: 'Do not be afraid'! Approach the Servant King who came not to be served but to serve; who gave His life that we might live.

FURTHER STUDY

Luke 1:26–38;
2 Tim. 1:2–5;
3:14–17

1. What might Jesus have learned from His mother's faith?

2. Reflect on Timothy's godly heritage.

Father God, thank You that I'm never far from Your thoughts, and that my name is written on the palm of Your hand. Help me this Christmas to be more aware of Your presence. Amen.

A Person, not a philosophy

FOR READING & MEDITATION – LUKE 2:1–12

'This will be a sign to you: You will find a baby wrapped in cloths and lying in a manger.' (v12)

This Christmas Day, we pause once again to reflect on the coming of Jesus into our sin-stained world. On the first Christmas morning, the announcement was made: 'You will find a baby…' This baby was a fact – an embodied fact. Even secular historians confirm the reality of the life of Jesus Christ.

There were many different cultures in the world at the time of the Saviour's coming, just as there are today. And if those cultures had felt they had a message to share with the world, they might have put it quite differently from the angel in today's passage. India may have said, 'You will find a mystic light'. Greece would have said, 'You will find a new wisdom and a new philosophical concept'. Rome would have said, 'You will find a new and more powerful imperialism'. But the angel of the Lord said, 'You will find a baby'. How amazing – how wonderful. The light that India yearned for, the wisdom Greece sought, the power Rome coveted, came together in a Person – Jesus. Religion was now realisation.

FURTHER STUDY

Isa. 9:2–7;
1 John 4:7–19

1. Reflect on Jesus in the light of Isaiah's vision.

2. Rejoice with John that love came down at Christmas.

This baby would grow into a man – and what a man! He has become the place of reconciliation where opposites meet. The material and the spiritual, after their long divorce, are reconciled in Him. The natural and the supernatural blend into His one life. Christianity, as so many people have come to understand, know and experience, is based not on a philosophy but on a Person. Not a rational ideology, but a relationship. This is the way it had to be. A distressed child isn't comforted with the idea of motherhood – it wants its mother. A sinful and distressed humanity could not be satisfied with the idea or philosophy of salvation. It needs a Saviour. Now we have one – Jesus.

Blessed Saviour, how I praise You once again on this Christmas Day for the glorious fact of Your birth into this world. Because I could not come to You, You came to me. My heart is Yours forever. Amen.

Fully forgiven

FOR READING & MEDITATION – 1 JOHN 1:1–10

*'If we confess our sins, he is faithful and just and will forgive us
our sins' (v9)*

We come now, not only to the last few days of this issue of *Every Day with Jesus*, but to the last few days of another year. What I would like to focus on over these few final days is that some are broken by the memory of sin – sin that God has forgiven, but wghich, for some reason, they are unable to put out of their minds. Over the years I have met many who, though they have gone to God for forgiveness, are still lacerated by the thought: how could I have ever done that? In reality this is a form of pride – a refusal to accept the fact that they could do such a thing.

This problem of not feeling forgiven plagues more people than we might realise. In my counselling days it was an issue that I had to deal with time and time again. But if a person has genuinely and sincerely asked God's forgiveness for some sin then, on the basis of today's text, that forgiveness is assured. If a person does not feel forgiven then, take it from me, something is going on in their personality that needs resolution. It could be a deeply ingrained belief, buried perhaps in the subconscious or unconscious, that they are too bad to be forgiven. It could be that they feel they need to add their own forgiveness to God's forgiveness – a form of legalism. Or there could be other dynamics going on that an experienced counsellor needs to help bring to the surface.

If what I am talking about is a problem you are experiencing, then I urge you to talk it over with a counsellor or a trusted friend. Whatever you do, don't let it linger. Sometimes just talking about the problem is the trigger that brings release.

FURTHER STUDY

1 Cor. 15:1–11;
Titus 2:9–14

1. Why did Paul's memory of sin not disable him?

2. How is Titus encouraged to connect with Christ's first and second coming?

Heavenly Father, help me understand and apply to my soul the deep meaning of forgiveness. If there is something blocking this then help me realise it and seek the help I need. In Jesus' name. Amen.

CWR's Find a Counsellor service can connect you to a local Waverley-trained counsellor in your local area. Visit www.cwr.org.uk/findacounsellor

The subtle nature of pride

FOR READING & MEDITATION – MATTHEW 15:1–20

'For out of the heart come evil thoughts, murder, adultery, sexual immorality, theft, false testimony, slander.' (v19)

In these last few days of the year we are thinking about how to recover from the brokenness caused by the memory of a past sin – a sin which God has forgiven but which still burns in our memory. How can we deal with this distressing situation?

First, we face and accept that the reason we still cling to the memory of some forgiven sin is almost certainly pride. As we said yesterday, it is a blow to our self-image. We cannot believe that we are capable of such a thing. That's pride – there is simply no other word for it.

FURTHER STUDY

Psa. 138:1–8;
Matt. 11:25–30

1. On whom does the exalted Lord look favourably?

2. Of what is Jesus our example?

Next we accept, as Jesus made clear in today's text, that despite all our outward respectability, there is within all of us an unrivalled self-interest at work that can, unless we are careful, lead us to do the most terrible things. We would like to think that we are not capable of destructive thoughts and actions, but the truth is, we are. Do you realise that Jesus was nailed to the cross because of our sin? Jesus was not done to death by a few sins perpetrated by monsters of iniquity. He was done to death by the same spirit that exists in your heart and mine – the spirit of rebellion against God. This spirit can manifest itself in many different ways, such as the bigotry of the Pharisees, the self-seeking of the Sadducees, the self-concern of Pilate, the censorious judgment of the crowd. These were the sins that led to Jesus' crucifixion, but all sin springs from one root cause: our pride and independence. That which put Jesus to death is in the heart of each one of us. If you can't say, 'There but for the grace of God go I,' then I suggest you may need to look again.

God, forgive me for my pride. I see how it can protect me from the true view of myself. Help me not just to recognise it but to deal with it by confessing it and turning away from it. In Jesus' name. Amen.

How even sin can be used

*'For sin shall not be your master, because you are not under law,
but under grace.' (v14)*

We have been seeing that those who struggle with the memory of sin which has already been forgiven may be doing so because of pride. Another thing I would say to those who find themselves in this situation is: remind yourself that God can do more with sin than just forgive it. That may be difficult for you to believe, but let me explain.

I heard an elderly minister make that statement when I was a young Christian, and at first I resisted it. I said to myself: 'How can God use sin? Surely it is His one intolerance?' Then, after a while, I saw what he meant. God does not want us to glory over our sin but He uses it to motivate us to achieve more in Him, to increase our compassion towards others and to show His tender heart for the fallen. We must be careful, of course, that we do not have the attitude Paul was countering when he said: 'Shall we go on sinning, so that grace may increase? By no means!' (vv1–2). If we sin in order that God may use it, then our reasoning is completely wrong. If, however, we commit sin, but then truly repent of it and take it to God in confession, not only will He forgive it but He will make something of it. Please do not think that I am saying sin is part of God's purposes – it isn't. But He can use our experiences to deepen our understanding of grace and put within us a longing to help others in their struggles.

Do you find this too difficult to take in? Then look to the cross. The crucifixion was one of the most devastating deeds ever committed, yet God used it to bring His redemption. It was our nadir – our lowest point – but it was God's zenith – His highest point. Blessed be His holy name for ever.

FURTHER STUDY

Eph. 2:1–7;
Heb. 10:15–25

1. Why will we be God's showcase for all eternity?

2. On what is our confidence before God based?

Father, I am so grateful that although You cannot condone sin, You can do more than forgive it. You can use my past experiences to warn me of its ever-present danger and keep me dependent on You. Amen.

Why do I do these things?

FOR READING & MEDITATION – EPHESIANS 1:1–14

'*In him we have redemption through his blood, the forgiveness of sins, in accordance with the riches of God's grace*' (v7)

We have been thinking about those who are broken by the memory of a sin that has been forgiven by God but which they brood over and cannot put behind them. We have been saying that the reason for this could be pride. They could be saying to themselves, 'How could *I* have ever done a thing like that?' (Notice the stress on the 'I'.) And this, we said, is a sign that they have too high an opinion of themselves – which is about as bad as having too low an opinion.

Now let's come to the important issue of forgiving oneself – something which seems to cause many people difficulty. I am convinced that people have difficulty forgiving themselves because they have some doubt about whether or not they have been truly forgiven by God. I am sure the two things are connected. If you harbour a doubt that God has forgiven you, when you have asked Him to do so and have come in true repentance before Him, then you must see that the doubt is really a denial. Instead of taking the words of Scripture that promise forgiveness (such as today's text), you are flinging them back into God's face, saying, 'I don't believe it.' You see, if you don't accept God's forgiveness, you will try to make your own atonement in the form of feelings of guilt and self-belittlement. Once you confess your sin, then as far as God is concerned, that's the end of it. Believe that – and act upon it. It's the gospel truth!

FURTHER STUDY

Psa. 130:1–8;
Eph. 4:32–5:2

1. How does the psalmist respond to being forgiven?

2. How can we show we have been forgiven?

If you are struggling in this area, then it might help to stand in front of a mirror with your Bible open at today's text. Reassure yourself that God has forgiven you, and say to yourself, by name: _____, God has forgiven you – now I forgive you too!

Gracious Father, although I understand many things, I fail so often to understand myself. Teach me more of what goes on deep inside me so that, being more self-aware, I may become more God-aware. For Your own dear name's sake. Amen.